P9-AOS-426

北海道
(札幌市)

青森県
(青森市)

秋田県
(秋田市)

岩手県
(盛岡市)

山形県
(山形市)

富山県
(富山市)

新潟県
(新潟市)

宮城県
(仙台市)

福島県
(福島市)

栃木県
(宇都宮市)

長野県
(長野市)

群馬県
(前橋市)

茨城県
(水戸市)

埼玉県
(さいたま市)

千葉県
(千葉市)

岐阜県
(岐阜市)

静岡県
(静岡市)

東京都
(東京)

知県
(屋市)

神奈川県
(横浜市)

山梨県
(甲府市)

0    100   200km

アルクの日本語テキスト ● ALC Press Japanese Textbook Series

# 日本事情入門

## View of Today's Japan

アルク 編　　佐々木瑞枝・著
by Mizue Sasaki

アルク

# はじめに

　日本語を勉強する外国人の方々は、「日本語」という言葉を勉強しながら、その背後にある「日本の文化」についても知りたいと思われるでしょう。

　日本はこの半世紀の間に大きく変わりました。人々の暮らし、考え方、経済・交通、日本人はどんな生活をし、どんなことに楽しみを見つけているのか、この本に紹介した内容は「現代日本社会」の断面です。

　昨年、ヨーロッパ各国の青年たちの「日本」に対するイメージ調査をしました。その時驚いたのは、日本についてのイメージが「着物、富士山、俳句」と「オートバイ、テレビ、過労死」といった両極端に交錯していて、本当の姿については「何も」といっていいくらい知られていなかったことです。

　この『日本事情入門』は、日本人の生活や考え方について基本的なことを、なるべくやさしい表現で説明してみました。たくさんのカラー写真が、きっと文章を理解する助けになると思います。

　世界の各地で日本語を勉強する方々のために英訳がついています。この本が、日本語の背景を知る上で皆さんの助けになれば幸いです。

1995年7月

佐々木瑞枝

# Foreword

I think that people from other countries who are studying the Japanese language might like to know more about the Japanese culture that forms the background for it.

Japan has changed greatly in this half-century, and this book presents a cross section of the present day Japanese society : Japanese lifestyles, thinking, economics and commerce, how people live and in what they find enjoyment.

Last year, in Europe, a survey was conducted investigating the image young people held of "Japan." What was surprising was that their image of Japan was a mixture of two extreme positions: "Kimono, Mount Fuji and Haiku" and "Motorcycles, Television and Death from Overwork." It is safe to say that about the true nature of Japan, they knew "Nothing."

In this book, "An introduction to Japanese Conditions", we explain as simply as we can, the fundamental points of Japanese daily life and thought. I am sure that the numerous color photographs will help in understanding the written explanations.

An English translation has been included in order that this book be understood everywhere around the world, and I will be extremely happy if the readers of this book find it somehow helpful in learning the background behind the Japanese language.

July 1995

Mizue Sasaki

# 目　次

# 日本の自然と季節
## Nature and the Seasons in Japan

四方を海にかこまれ、北海道から沖縄まで南北に長い日本列島の自然は変化に富んでいます。春・夏・秋・冬、季節とともに自然の色もさまざまにかわります。

The Japanese archipelago, running from Hokkaido in the north to Okinawa in the south, surrounded in all directions by water, boasts of a nature rich in variety. With each changing season - spring, summer, autumn, and winter - the colors of the landscape also change.

山

日本は山地が多い。連なった高い峰、木は茂って森となり、すぐれた自然環境になっている
←朝の穂高連峰（長野県）

川

陸地の幅がせまく、山から海にそそぐ川の流れは急ではやい。清流ではアユなどの魚が釣れる
菊地渓谷（熊本県）→

青い海と空、岩にうちよせる波と白い砂、松のみどり、美しい海岸が日本のいたるところで見られる
←堂ヶ島海岸（静岡県）

海

5

## 春

さくらは日本の花の代
表。人びとは満開のさく
らの下で花見をたのしむ
（福島・花見山　4月）

## 夏

明るい太陽に向かって、
いっせいに花開いたひ
まわり。（北海道・北竜
町のひまわり畑　8月）

## 秋

木の葉が赤や黄色に色づ
く季節。山はだはもみじ
のじゅうたんになる
（長野・乗鞍岳　10月）

## 冬

きびしい寒さのおとずれ
とともに気温が下がり、
枝に霧氷の花がさく
（長野・美ヶ原　2月）

# <ruby>日<rt>に</rt></ruby><ruby>本<rt>ほん</rt></ruby><ruby>人<rt>じん</rt></ruby>の<ruby>生<rt>せい</rt></ruby><ruby>活<rt>かつ</rt></ruby>
## The Life of the Japanese

<ruby>服装<rt>ふくそう</rt></ruby>・<ruby>食事<rt>しょくじ</rt></ruby>・<ruby>住<rt>す</rt></ruby>まい、<ruby>生活全体<rt>せいかつぜんたい</rt></ruby>にわたって、<ruby>今<rt>いま</rt></ruby>の<ruby>日本人<rt>にほんじん</rt></ruby>は<ruby>伝統的<rt>でんとうてき</rt></ruby>な<ruby>日本独特<rt>にほんどくとく</rt></ruby>のもの、<ruby>外国<rt>がいこく</rt></ruby>から<ruby>伝<rt>つた</rt></ruby>わってきたもの、この<ruby>和風<rt>わふう</rt></ruby>と<ruby>洋風<rt>ようふう</rt></ruby>の<ruby>両方<rt>りょうほう</rt></ruby>を<ruby>取<rt>と</rt></ruby>り<ruby>入<rt>い</rt></ruby>れて<ruby>暮<rt>く</rt></ruby>らしています。

In every aspect of daily life, the Japanese of today put to use both Japanese elements that are unique to traditional Japan, and Western elements that were brought over from across the ocean-from clothing to food to housing.

● ● ● ●  ● ● ● ●

## <ruby>衣<rt>い</rt></ruby>

<ruby>ふだんの服装<rt>ふくそう</rt></ruby>は<ruby>洋服<rt>ようふく</rt></ruby>が<ruby>多<rt>おお</rt></ruby>く、<ruby>着物<rt>きもの</rt></ruby>を<ruby>着<rt>き</rt></ruby>る<ruby>機会<rt>きかい</rt></ruby>は、だんだん<ruby>少<rt>すく</rt></ruby>なくなってきた

▲<ruby>かんたんに<ruby>着<rt>き</rt></ruby>られる<ruby>夏<rt>なつ</rt></ruby>の<ruby>浴衣<rt>ゆかた</rt></ruby>は<ruby>子<rt>こ</rt></ruby>どもにも<ruby>人気<rt>にんき</rt></ruby>がある

▶
<ruby>七五三<rt>しちごさん</rt></ruby>には<ruby>着<rt>き</rt></ruby>かざって<ruby>神社<rt>じんじゃ</rt></ruby>へおまいりする

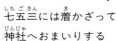

<ruby>着物<rt>きもの</rt></ruby>を<ruby>着<rt>き</rt></ruby>たときは、たびをはき、ぞうりをはく

若者たちのファッションは流行を取り入れながらも自由で個性的だ

シャツ・セーターにパンツ。カジュアルな服装がめだつ。Tシャツにジーンズは男女に共通のファッション

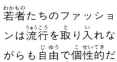

## 若者のファッション
## 制服

小学生。ぼうし、ランドセル、くつした、くつまでおそろい

中学生。同じ学校の男子、女子でそれぞれ制服がきめられている。制服がなく、服装が自由な学校もある

銀行、デパートなど、女性の多い職場には制服がある

# 日本の自然と季節

日本には四季があります。春、夏、秋、冬、日本人はそれぞれの季節を大切にして暮らしています。

## ■春

春、3月から4月、5月にかけては、梅や桜、つつじの花が日本列島を美しくいろどります。季節ごとに美しい花を見るのはうれしいことです。桜は日本で一番暖かい沖縄から咲き始め、約2か月かけて北の北海道まで達します。これは桜前線と呼ばれています。図を見ると、桜のさいていくようすがわかりますね。

晩春から初夏にかけて、北海道をのぞき、日本は梅雨の季節に入ります。梅雨の季節は約40日間で、気象庁がテレビやラジオで、「梅雨入り宣言」、「梅雨明け宣言」をします。これは日本独特のものです。農家の人たちにとって、梅雨は大切な季節です。あまり雨が降らない時は「空梅雨」と言われ、米の収穫に影響してきます。また、水源地であるダムや川の水が少なくなって、水道が断水するなど、都会の生活にも影響が出てきます。

## ■夏

7月の中旬に梅雨があけると、真夏の太陽が輝き、気温が30度以上になる「真夏日」が続きます。南の九州では約2か月間、東京では約45日、京都は盆地にあるために風の通りが悪く、約68日も続きます。日本の夏は湿度も非常に高いため、とても過ごしにくく、涼しい北海道や日本の各地の高原地帯は避暑に来た人たちでにぎわいます。

電車やバス、デパートやスーパー、レストランや会社、ほとんどの場所にエアコンがあるので、外との温度差ははげしく、外出には上着が必要です。

8月から9月にかけて、台風が日本をおそいます。大型台風になると風速40メートル以上、各地に集中的に雨が降り、洪水や崖くずれ、家屋の浸水がおきるなどの被害が出ます。テレビのニュースでも「台風の進路にあたるところは十分に警戒してください」と、一晩中、台風情報を流

## Nature and the Seasons in Japan

Japan has four distinct seasons: spring, summer, autumn and winter. Each season has its own important part to play in the lives of the Japanese people.

### Spring

Spring, lasting from March through April into May is a time when plum, cherry and azalea blossoms are gloriously in bloom throughout the Japanese archipelago. People look forward to the beautiful flowers that each new season brings. Cherry blossoms begin to bloom in Okinawa, where it is warmer and, over a period of two months, continue to bloom as far north as Hokkaido. The gradual movement north of the blossoming cherries is referred to as the sakura zensen or 'cherry blossom front'. When you look at a map, it is possible to appreciate this movement of the cherry blossoms.

From late spring into early summer, Japan, with the exception of Hokkaido, experiences the rainy season. The Meteorological Agency makes announcements on TV and radio, officially declaring the beginning and end of the rainy season, which usually lasts for about forty days. This is a phenomenon peculiar to Japan. The rainy season is an important season for people working in agriculture. People use the expression karatsuyu to refer to a year when only a small amount of rain falls. Lack of rain invariably affects the rice harvest.

Low rainfall may also affect the lives of those living in the cities, since low water levels in dams and rivers which provide the water supply may lead to the imposition of water restrictions.

### Summer

After the rainy season ends in the middle of July, the summer sun beats down, temperatures climb into the thirties and the days of high summer begin. The length of summer varies from area to area: Kyushu in the south, approximately two months, Tokyo, about forty-five days, while Kyoto, because it is located in a basin and doesn't receive fresh breezes, has 68 days of summer. The extremely high temperatures of the Japanese summer make it uncomfortable for day-to-day life. Consequently, people throng to cooler areas, such as Hokkaido and the various highlands to escape the heat.

As the use of air-conditioners is widespread, whether it be on trains, buses, in department stores, in supermarkets, in restaurants or in the companies, it becomes necessary to carry a jacket to guard against the sudden temperature differences.

From August to September it is typhoon season in Japan. When typhoons reach a large size and wind velocities exceed 40 metres per second, there can be localized torrential downpours, flooding and landslides, causing houses to be inundated, with much damage resulting. Television news programmes issue continuous bulletins throughout the night, urging people to

しつづけます。飛行機や列車といった交通もストップすることがあります。アメリカにはハリケーンがありますが、日本と同じような温帯気候のヨーロッパには台風がなく、台風を経験したことのない留学生にとっては「驚きの数日間」を過ごすことになります。台風の翌日は「台風一過」といって空は晴れ上がり、前日の天気がうそのようです。

## ■秋

8月の終わり頃になると、気温は下がりはじめ「秋雨」の後、待望の秋を迎えます。暑い夏の後にくる秋はさわやかで心地良く「スポーツの秋」「食欲の秋」「勉学の秋」などという言葉で言われます。木々は赤や黄色の美しい装いをこらし「紅葉前線」が、北から南へと移動します。「紅葉の名所」はどこも「紅葉狩り」の人々にぎわいます。

## ■冬

11月の中旬に日本海側で初雪が降り、徐々に日本は冬に向かっていきます。日本の冬の特徴は、太平洋側は冷たく乾いた「からっかぜ」が吹き、天気の良い日が多く、日本海側では大雪が降ることでしょう。富山県などの雪の多い地方では2メートル以上の雪が積もり、屋根の雪下ろしが大切な仕事になっています。若者たちが都市に集中し、老人の多い過疎地帯になってしまったところでは、アルバイトをやとって雪下ろしをするので大変です。

冬はウインタースポーツの代表であるスキーが楽しめる時です。志賀高原、蔵王、苗場といったスキーのメッカには、カラフルなスキーウエアの若者たちが集まります。土曜日や日曜日、年末・年始といった休日には、リフトやロープ・ウエーに長い列ができます。

日本語には「冬来たりなば、春遠からじ」という言葉があります。1月、2月と寒い季節に耐え、3月の春の訪れを待ちます。地球上には同緯度の国がたくさんあります。日本にこのような四季があるのは、地形、海流、季節風の変化などに影響を受けているからでしょう。

日本の季節の変化は、日本の衣食住、農業、年中行事などに大きく関係しています。外国の方々も、日本にきたら、日本の四季を楽しんでください。

## Autumn

take note of the areas which fall in the path of the advancing typhoon and to take every precaution necessary. Transportation, including planes and trains, may be disrupted at such times. America has its hurricanes. However, in Europe, which has a temperate climate similar to that of Japan, there are no typhoons. Consequently, foreign students who have experienced a typhoon in Japan for the first time have found it to be an 'alarming few days'. The day after a typhoon has passed through is known as taifuu ikka and this time is associated with perfectly clear blue skies-- the weather of the previous day as if imagined.

## Autumn

Towards the end of August temperatures begin to drop and after the autumn rains the long-awaited season of autumn is ushered in. After the sweltering heat of summer, autumn feels refreshing and pleasant and is referred to variously as 'autumn, the season for sports, the season for having a hearty appetite and the season for study'. With the trees a blaze of reds and yellows, the 'autumnal colours front' moves from the north towards the south. People anxious to view the autumn colours at their best flock to places renowned for their spectacular autumnal tints.

## Winter

The first snows of the season fall on the Japan Sea side of the country around the middle of November, heralding the gradual approach of winter. The Japanese winter may be said to have the following characteristics: on the Pacific Coast side, cold, dry winds blow and there are many fine days, while on the Japan Sea side there is heavy snowfall. In areas which receive heavy snowfall, such as Toyama Prefecture,snow may reach a depth of over 2 metres. Consequently, removal of snow from the roofs of houses is an important task. Since young people are gravitating towards big cities, it is becoming difficult to employ part-time workers to help with snow removal in depopulated areas which have large numbers of old people.

Winter is the time for skiing--a common winter sport. Young skiers dressed in colourful ski wear can be seen in well-known skiing areas such as Shiga Heights, Zao and Naeba. Long queues form at ski lifts and ropeways on holidays--especially on Saturdays and Sundays and during the New Year holiday period.

In Japanese there is a saying 'If Winter comes, can Spring be far behind?' In other words, we endure the cold of January and February, in anticipation of the coming of spring in March.

There are many countries in the world located at the same latitude as Japan. Japan owes its distinctive seasons to perhaps a number of influences--topography, ocean currents and variations in seasonal winds.

The changes of the seasons in Japan bear a close relationship to the food, clothing and housing, agriculture and annual events that are held.

May foreign visitors to Japan be able to appreciate the changes that each season brings!

# 日本人の生活

## ●●●衣●●●

　日本の衣服というと、すぐ着物を思い浮かべるかもしれません。しかし、日本人が着物を着るのは、成人式、結婚式、入学式といったごく限られた機会で、それも女性が多く、ふだんは洋服で過ごすことが多いのです。明治時代、日本に洋服が輸入されて以来、洋服が着物よりも活動的なことから、だんだん洋服が着られるようになりました。今では若者は男女を問わずジーンズ姿が圧倒的です。

　着物は洋服に対して「和服」とも言われます。和服は長方形の布を縫って作られた直線的な衣服です。人間には、背の高い人、低い人、太っている人、やせている人とさまざまですが、体型が多少違っても同じ着物ですみます。サイズに関係なく、融通性があるということが着物の良さでしょう。着物は体を包む風呂敷と考えてもよいかもしれません。成人式や結婚式に着る着物はとても値段が高く、中には数百万円するものもあります。しかし、色や柄に気をつければ、体格が少々変わっても何年にもわたって着ることができます。日本の民族衣装でありながら、着物姿を見るのはだんだん少なくなってきています。着るのがむずかしい、着ていて苦しくリラックスできない、値段が高いなど、いろいろな要素が、着られなくなっていく原因です。

　着物で一番着られているのは、浴衣です。浴衣は木綿でできた夏用の着物です。ほとんどの着物が絹でできているのに比べると、浴衣は値段も安く、洗濯も楽です。子ども時代に「盆踊り」の時、浴衣を着たことがある人が多いようです。着物を着る時の履物はぞうりか下駄ですが、浴衣を着る時には、下駄をはきます。日本では1950年代くらいまでは、下駄は一般的な日本人の普段着の時の履物でした。町には必ず下駄やさんがあって、職人さんが下駄を作っていたものです。今では下駄やさんは、ほとんど姿を消してしまいました。日本が西欧化していく中で、伝統的な日本

## Clothing

When you refer to Japanese clothing it may be the kimono which immediately springs to mind. However, the number of occasions when people wear kimono is extremely limited. For example, at coming-of-age ceremonies, weddings and school entrance ceremonies. At these times, it is mostly women who wear kimono. Generally, people wear Western-style clothing for everyday wear.

Since Western-style clothing was introduced into Japan during the Meiji Era, the wearing of Western clothes, with their dynamic appearance, rather than traditional kimono, has gradually been becoming more popular. These days, the sight of young people, irrespective of gender, wearing jeans is an extremely common one.

Kimono, as opposed to Western-style clothing, is also referred to as wafuku ('Japanese clothes'). Japanese clothing is stitched in straight lines from a rectangular piece of cloth. People come in all shapes and sizes--tall, short, fat and thin. Even if people's figures change slightly, they will still be able to make do with the same kimono. Thus, perhaps the strong-point of the kimono is the fact that it retains its versatility, regardless of the size of the wearer. The kimono may be viewed as a kind of wrapping cloth for the body.

The kimono worn at coming-of-age and wedding ceremonies are very expensive and may cost as much as several million yen. However, if care is exercized with regards to the selection of colour and pattern, kimono may be worn for many years, even if there are slight changes in physique. Despite the fact that it is recognized as the folk costume of Japan, the wearing of the kimono is becoming an increasingly rare sight. Being difficult to put on, uncomfortable to wear and hard to relax in and also being exhorbitant in price are factors that contribute to the reason for fewer and fewer pople wearing kimono today.

The most commonly worn item of Japanese clothing is the yukata. This is a kimono made of cotton for summer wear. Compared to kimono which are mostly made of silk, the yukata is inexpensive and easy to wash. Most people can probably remember a time in their childhood when they dressed up in yukata to dance in the Bon Festival.

When wearing kimono, sandals (zori) or wooden clogs (geta) are worn on the feet, however, only geta are worn with yukata. Until about the 1950's geta were considered the norm for footwear for the Japanese people. Each town would invariably have a number of geta merchants and craftsmen who would make the clogs by hand. These days, geta merchants have almost entirely disappeared . It is unfortunate that, as Japan becomes increasingly

の文化が少しずつ消えていくのは、残念です。

　衣服にはさまざまな役割があります。まず、自然環境への適応ということでしょう。暑さ、寒さ、光、水分、風、などから体をまもるためです。「人間と動物の違いは、服を着るか着ないかだ」とも言えます。

　衣服を「文化」としての視点から見ると、次の4つにまとめることができます。

## 1．装飾のため

　いつも美しくいたいというのは、人間の欲求でしょう。しかし時代や年代によって「美」の考え方が違うのは当然です。たとえば、ひざのすりきれたジーンズを、「かっこいい」とする若者と、「汚らしい」と思う大人がいるのは、どこの国にも共通して見られることです。

## 2．社会的な身分や地位を象徴するという役目

　戦前（第2次世界大戦前）は日本はもっと身分がはっきりした社会でした。会社員か職人さんかは、その服装を見るだけでわかりました。しかし、今では、誰もが同じような服装をしているために、服装から身分を判断することはむずかしいのです。

## 3．ある組織・集団に所属していることを示す

　制服や軍服がその代表でしょう。日本では、制服は幼稚園から高校を卒業するまでつきまとい、場合によっては、会社に入っても制服を着なければなりません。

## 4．儀礼としてのしるし

　衣服は民族としての風俗や儀礼の大切な要素でもあります。ふだんとは違った服装をすることで、儀礼の重要性を感じさせるからです。日本では七五三といって、7歳、5歳、3歳の時や20歳の成人式に着る着物、60歳の還暦に着る赤いチャンチャンコ（ベストに似たもの）など、人生の大切な時期に特別な服装をします。日本は世界で一番の長寿国になりました。「60歳はまだ働きざかり。まだ、赤いチャンチャンコは早い」といやがる人もいます。

　都会と農村、若者と老人、外出着と普段着、通勤用とレジャー用、春夏秋冬、時と場合によって、日本人は衣服を使い分けています。

Westernized, it is gradually losing parts of its traditional culture.

Clothing serves various functions. Firstly, it helps us in adapting to our natural surroundings. Clothing protects our bodies from heat, cold, light, moisture, wind and so on. It is said that what separates human beings from animals is the fact that human beings wear clothes.

When clothing is examined from the viewpoint of 'culture', it may be observed as fulfilling a number of functions.

(1) The function of adornment. The constant wish to be 'beautiful' is perhaps a human desire. However, depending on the era or period, it is only natural to think that what is construed as being 'beautiful' may vary from person to person. For example, tha fact that some young people consider wearing jeans which are worn-out at the knees 'smart', while some adults would consider the same 'dirty-looking', would be a commonly held perception in many countries.

(2) The role of symbolizing a person's social status or position. Before the Second World War, Japan was very much more a status-conscious society. Judging by the clothing worn, one could tell whether a person was a company employee or a craftsman. These days, however, it is difficult to judge a person's status based upon appearances, since all people tend to dress in the same way.

(3) The function of identifying a particular organization or group to which a person belongs. Uniforms and military attire would be good examples of this role of clothing. In Japan, the wearing of uniforms continues from kindergarten until the end of high school and, in some cases, may be required even after joining a company.

(4) A sign of etiquette. Clothing constitutes an important element of the customs or etiquette of the people. This is because, by wearing clothes which are different from what one would normally wear, one is able to impress on others the importance of etiquette. In Japan, special clothing is worn at important times of one's life. For example, when children reach the ages of three, five or seven, and when young people attain the age of twenty, special kimono are worn. When someone reaches the auspicious age of sixty, a red padded vest called a chanchanko may be worn. Japan has become the country with the highest rate of longevity in the world. So, it is not uncommon to find people who grudgingly declare "At sixty, I'm still in my working prime. It's too early for me to be wearing a chanchanko."

The clothing Japanese people wear varies depending on numerous factors: whether it is the city or a farming village, whether the people are young or elderly, whether street clothes are being worn or everyday wear is, whether a person is commuting to work or wearing clothing for leisure and, what season or time it is, will all have some bearing on the situation.

▲食料品しょくりょうひんを売うる店みせ。いろいろな野菜やさい
や果物くだものを売うっている八百屋やおや

◀
▶
魚さかなや貝かいなどの海産物かいさんぶつを売うる
魚屋さかなや。並ならべた魚さかなに名前なまえと値ね
段だんがつけてある

豆腐屋とうふや。大豆だいずを原料げんりょうにした豆腐とうふは
日本人にほんじんが好すきな食品しょくひん。「みそ汁しる」や
「すきやき」に欠かかせない

▼食堂しょくどうのショーケースには、和食わしょく、
洋食ようしょく、中華料理ちゅうかりょうりなど、いろいろな
メニューの見本みほんがならぶ

ごはん、みそ汁、焼き魚、つけものなど、一般的な日本の家庭料理

お昼の食事はそばやラーメンなどで軽くすませる場合が多い

デパートやスーパーのおべんとう売り場。どれにしようか？

おかず売り場は種類も多く、小人数にも向くので便利

すしは世界で通用するようになった日本料理の代表。すしやさしみとして、人気の高いマグロ（東京・築地の市場）

日本の住宅の内部。畳を敷いた部屋はふすまや障子で仕切られている。障子の外側は板敷きの縁側で、庭に面して、ガラス戸が入れてある

縁側は庭から直接出入りできる。日のあたる縁側はいこいの場所にもなる（左）

雨風を防ぎ、防犯のため、夜になると雨戸をしめる（右）

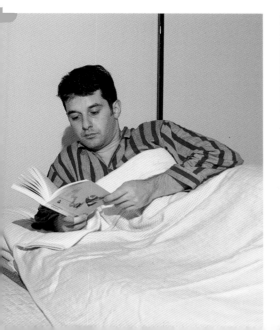

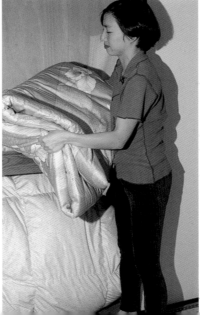

夜、寝るときは畳の上にふとんを敷く（左）

朝、起きると、ふとんは押し入れにしまう（右）

15

洋風のダイニング・キッチンは便利さから、日本家屋にも取り入れられている

都会はコンクリート製のマンションやアパートが多くなった

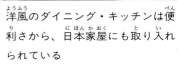

整った環境に建つ新しい住宅（住都公団の集合住宅）

# ●●●食●●●

日本でテレビを見ていると、食べ物に関する番組が非常に多いことがわかります。どのチャンネルでも、1日に3つくらいの料理番組があるのですから。

現代の日本は「飽食の時代」と言われ、世界のあらゆる料理が食べられます。日本料理、中国料理、インド料理、韓国料理、ギリシャ料理、イタリア料理、例をあげればきりがありません。

家庭でも、朝はトーストにハムエッグ、昼はそばを食べ、夕食には中華料理を食べる、こんな家庭が多いのではないでしょうか。地域や年代によって、多少の差はあるにしても、和食だけ、洋食だけというよりは、このようにさまざまな料理を組み合わせて食べるというのが、現代の日本人の食生活だといえます。

食事には、2つの目的があります。栄養をとること、そして楽しむことです。とくに成長期にはバランスの良い栄養が必要です。小学校や一部の中学校では学校給食がありますが、統計によると「給食はおいしくない」という生徒が増えてきています。

今は全員が教室で、限られた時間に、同じメニューの画一的な食事をしています。これをカフェテリア方式にして食べたいものを選ばせる、教室で食べさせるのではなく食堂を準備する、食事の時間を十分にとるなど、いろいろな点で学校給食のあり方を考え直す時期にきているのかもしれません。

歴史的にみると、日本人の食事は、高度成長期をさかいに大きな変化が起きています。

1960年代に、農村から都会に出て働く若者が増え、都市に人口が集中しました。その結果、野菜や果物、魚といったものが、生産地から遠距離の都市へ運ばれることになりました。保存と輸送の必要性から、野菜も果物も規格にあった大きさのものが、まるで工業製品のように、ダンボール箱やプラスティックのケースに入れられて運ばれるようになりました。魚や肉や卵にしても同じです。

## Food

Watching television in Japan, you will observe that there are an extemely large number of programmes related to 'food'. Whatever the channel, you can guarantee that at least three 'cooking programmes' will be aired every day.

Present-day Japan is said to be experiencing an 'age of gluttony', and it is indeed possible to enjoy the food of countries from all over the world. The variety is seemingly endless--Japanese, Chinese, Indian, Korean, Greek and Italian cuisine are all available.

There are probably many families who would enjoy toast with ham and eggs for breakfast, buckwheat noodles for lunch and Chinese food for dinner. It could be said that Japanese people these days enjoy a diet which consists of a combination of various styles of cooking, and is not exclusively Japanese or Western, given certain variation depending upon region or age-group.

Meals fulfil two purposes. They supply nutrition and they also provide a certain amount of enjoyment. During a period of physical growth it is particularly important to maintain a good nutritional balance. In primary schools and certain junior highschools, school lunches are served, however, statistics show that the number of students who find school lunches to be 'not nice' is on the increase.

At present, all students eat a standard single menu meal in their classrooms at a set time. The school lunch service is entering a period of reassessment. Would it be better to have a caffeteria-style system, where students choose what they want to eat? Rather than having students eat in classrooms would it be better to provide a dining-hall? Should students be provided with more time in which to enjoy meals? These are but a few of the questions under consideration.

Historically speaking, the diet of the Japanese people began to undergo great change from the time of Japan's rapid economic growth period.

During the 1960's the numbers of young people leaving farming communities for the big cities, in search of work, increased dramatically, causing the populations of cities to swell. As a result, it became necessary for vegetables, fruit and fish to be transported long distances from producing areas to the cities. Consequently, to meet this demand for preservation and transportation, fruit and vegetables have come to be packed in plastic cases or cardboard boxes, having been selected to meet the standard required size before being shipped, just as if they were a kind of industrial product. This situation is also the same with fish, meat and eggs.

Today, the mainstream of young people have switched their interest in food away

そして、鮮度や季節感を楽しむ日本の家庭料理から、ハンバーグやスパゲティー、焼き肉といった、季節を問わずいつでも食べられるものへと、若者たちの食事の主流が移ってきています。

また、大家族から核家族へと変わっていくにつれて、毎日ご飯をたき、おかずを作るという主婦の仕事は、だんだん少なくなってきました。夕方買い物に行き、家族のために夕食の支度をするということは、いまだに主婦の仕事の中で大きなウエートを占めています。しかし、大型冷蔵庫が家庭に行き渡ったことから、毎日買い物に行く必要はなくなりました。また、働く女性が増えて、パート勤めの主婦が帰りにスーパーで半製品になったおかずを買うというのも、日常見られる光景です。

デパートなどのおかず売り場には、小所帯の人でも、手軽に買えるおかずがたくさん並び、夕方はとても混雑します。値段が手頃で、切ったり煮たりする必要がなく、味もまあまあというのが、人気の秘密でしょうか。その結果、「わが家の味」「お母さんの味」といったものが、失われていく傾向にあります。

家族が外で食事をする機会も増えています。ファミリーレストランの増加は、日本人の食べ物に対する指向が、画一化されたことの、1つの具体例と言えそうです。

グルメブームは、そうした画一化の裏返しの現象と言えるでしょう。「少しでも新鮮なものを材料に」ということで、産地から都会へと、高速道路を冷凍車が魚やカニを積んで運びます。

ぜいたくな食事の楽しみ方と言えますが、1回の食事が数万円するレストランも、有名なシェフのいる店は、かなり早くから予約しないと席がとれません。

こうしたレストランに人気が集中するのも、子どもの頃から画一化された給食で育ち、ファミリーレストランの味にならされて育った年代が自分の好みの味を求める時代になったということでしょうか。

from traditional Japanese home cooking, which allows people to savour the degree of freshness and the sense of the seasons, towards food which is unaffected by seasonality and can be eaten at any time, such as hamburger steaks, spaghetti and grilled meat.

With the shift in society from large families to nuclear families, the tasks of housewives of cooking rice and preparing side dishes every day have also gradually been changing. Going shopping in the evening and preparing dinner for the family still constitutes an important part of a housewife's role. However, the increasing use of large refrigerators has meant that there is no longer the need to go shopping every day. What with increasing numbers of working women, seeing housewives who, at the same time are managing to hold down part-time jobs, shopping in supermarkets for semi-prepared food to go with the main meal, is a familiar sight.

In the evenings, counters at department stores selling pre-prepared side dishes are jammed with customers, often people from small families, anxious to buy the readily available foodstuffs on display. Reasonably priced, no need to cut or boil and not tasting too bad--perhaps these are the secrets of the popularity of such food items. Consequently, the concepts of 'home cooking' and 'mother's cooking' are tending to disappear.

Families are eating out more often. The fact that the number of so-called 'family restaurants' has boomed could be said to be a clear example of how uniform the diet of Japanese people has become and what direction it is moving in.

The recent 'gourmet boom' could be interpreted as being a kind of reaction against such uniformity. To cater for the tastes of those who 'would like to try something made with extra fresh ingredients', fish, crab and the like are caught fresh and brought via expressway in refrigerated vehicles to the cities. This kind of dining may be viewed as an extravagance and yet, without booking well in advance, it can become difficult to secure a table in establishments which employ famous chefs and can ask for tens of thousands of yen for a single meal.

Perhaps a further reason that this style of reataurant is attracting such popularity is that a generation of people who have been brought up on uniform school meals and have been conditioned by 'family restaurant'- style food, have come to the stage where they want something that suits their own tastes.

# ●●●住●●●

日本の首都である東京は、敗戦によって焼け野原となり、その後、都市計画もないままに、マンモス化して出来上がりました。パリのようにビルの高さに規制があり、まるで整然とした1枚の絵のような感じは、東京にはありません。新しい高層ビルの間に古い2階建ての日本家屋があったり、町並みはデコボコしていて、雑然としています。

しかし、1000万人もの人間が住む大都会でありながら、女性が夜も1人で歩ける安全さ、地下鉄が縦横に走り、どこにでも簡単に行けること、買いたいものは何でも手に入ることなど、東京に一度住んだら、その便利さ、快適さに、とてもほかの所に住む気持ちにはなれません。

新幹線に乗って東京をはなれると、ビルの代わりに日本家屋が多くなってきます。黒い瓦屋根が、広がる田園風景の中に、見事に溶け込んでいます。昔ながらの日本の住宅は木造建築で、コンクリートでできたビルにくらべると、自然の暖かみが感じられます。四季の変化に富む日本では、春と秋は快適な季節です。しかし、蒸し暑い夏には、通風の良いことが大切な条件になります。コンクリートのビルが閉鎖的なのにくらべると、日本の家屋はずっと開放的で、窓が多く、風が吹き抜けやすくなっています。しかし、冬には機密性がないことから、いくら暖房しても、どこからか冷たい風が入ってきます。暖房もない昔の人たちは、よくがまんできたものだと、感心してしまいます。

平均的な日本家屋を見てみましょう。家には和室がいくつかと風呂場、台所、庭があり、部屋の仕切りはふすまや障子です。夜は木でできた雨戸を閉めます。数十年前は、夜になると雨戸をしめ、朝になると開けるのが大部分の日本人の毎日の習慣でした。

日本の家屋の特徴は、家にあがる時に履物を脱ぐことです。韓国、イラン、トルコでも見られるようですが、この習慣は世界にあまり例がないようです。

縁側は、冬の暖かい日に、ひなたぼっこしたり、近所の人がたずねてきた時には、そこに腰掛けて一緒に話すなど、

## Housing

Tokyo, the capital city of present-day Japan, reduced to a vast expanse of burnt ruins after the defeat of the Second World War, has grown to become the megalopolis it is today, with little attention having been paid to urban planning. Tokyo is very unlike a city like Paris, for example, with its regulated building height and almost picture-like impression of orderliness. In Tokyo, one can find old two-storied traditional Japanese houses nestled between new high-rise buildings--the unevenness of the rows of houses and stores conveying a feeling of disorder.

Despite being a huge city with a population of ten million people, once you have lived in Tokyo and experienced the convenience and comfort of the city, it can almost become difficult to settle elsewhere. Being safe for women to walk alone at night; having an extensive subway network to facilitate travel within the city and the availability of any kind of merchandise for purchase--these are some of the reasons for Tokyo being a popular place to live.

When you head out of Tokyo on the Bullet Train, buildings are soon replaced by increasing numbers of Japanese houses. Black tiled roofs are perfectly integrated into the vast rural landscape. Traditional Japanese houses have been constructed of wood since olden times and, compared to concrete buildings, reflect a natural warmth. In Japan, with its many changes in the seasons, spring and autumn are regarded as being 'pleasant' seasons. Summer, however, is a different matter. An important condition for coping with the humid summer is good ventilation. Compared to the 'closed-in' feeling of buildings built with concrete, Japanese houses are much more open--there are many windows, allowing free access to fresh breezes. In winter, however, since houses are not airtight, no amount of heating seems to be able to rid the rooms of cold draughts. One cannot help but admire the fortitude of the people of bygone eras--people to whom 'heating' was unknown.

Let us examine the typical traditional Japanese house. Usually there will be a number of Japanese rooms, which are divided by sliding doors and screens, a bathroom, a kitchen and a garden. At night the wooden storm shutters on the windows are closed. In fact, thirty or forty years ago, closing the storm shutters in the evening and opening them once again in the morning would have been the daily practice of most Japanese families.

The removal of one's shoes before entering the house is a characteristic of Japanese houses. This custom, also practised in Korea, Iran and Turkey, is mostly unknown in other parts of the world.

The verandah of the traditional Japanese house has a variety of useful functions. It can be used as a place for basking in the sun on warm winter days. When neighbours call, it is a handy place to sit and have a conversation--neither inside the house, nor outside, the verandah serves as a kind of midway point, being particularly convenient for those conver-

家の内と外の中間的な性格を持っています。家にあがって話すほどではないけれど、外では話しにくい、こんな時に縁側はとても便利な存在と言えるでしょう。

　和室は食事の時には食堂になり、寝る時には布団を敷いて寝室に変わります。和室にはたいてい押し入れがついていて、夜になるとふとんをしき、朝になると畳んでしまいます。和室はベッドと違って、いくつもの布団が敷けますから、何人もの人が一緒に寝ることができます。また、客室に使う和室には床の間があって、そこには掛け軸や生け花が飾られます。

　日本家屋の構造は、個人のプライバシーが保てない、食事する場所と寝る場所が同じなのは不便、などという別の理由から、最近は小さな個室を持った住宅が増えてきました。核家族が増え、ライフスタイルが変化してきたことで、それまでの日本家屋が住みにくくなってきたのです。

　今、日本の各地に次々と建てられているマンションやアパートは２ＤＫ（部屋が二つにダイニング・キッチン）や３ＤＫ、３ＬＤＫ（リビングルームがくわわる）など、いろいろなタイプのものがあります。洋風の椅子の生活でも、和室が一部屋は欲しいと思う人が多いのでしょうか。マンションには床の間のある和室がついていることも、珍しくありません。和洋折衷というところですね。

　機密性に富んだ建物では、当然冷房や暖房がよくきき、季節の移り変わりにもだんだん鈍感になってしまいます。日本家屋なら、洗濯物を干したり、庭の手入れをする時に気軽に隣の人と話せたのに、アパートでは隣、近所の人と顔を合わせる機会も少なくなります。住宅の変化が、人間社会に与える影響は本当に大きいと言えます。

　家は洋服などと違って、気軽に取り替えるわけにはいきません。一度家を建てると、まわりの環境や家の構造によって、私たちの生活は大きく変化します。これだけ多くの規格化されたアパートに住む人が増えることによって、日本の社会はどのように変化していくのでしょうか。

sations which would be difficult to hold outside, and yet do not necessitate going inside the house.

A Japanese-style room can become a dining room at meal times, and when it comes time to sleep, the bedding can be laid out, transforming the room into a bedroom. Japanese-style rooms usually have a closet used to store bedding--at night the bedding ('bedding') is laid out and in the morning, it is folded up and put away. Unlike a Western-style room with beds, the Japanese-style room may be used to accommodate a number of futon, allowing several people to share the room--a most convenient feature. The Japanese-style room, which may also be used as a guest room, has a **tokonoma** ('recessed alcove'), often decorated by a hanging scroll or **ikebana** display.

Since the layout of traditional houses affords the individual little privacy and due to the inconvenience of the fact that eating and sleeping occur in the same place, these days the number of houses with small, individual rooms is on the increase. The growing numbers of nuclear families, with the accompanying changes in lifestyle, has meant that the traditional Japanese house no longer offers the living comfort sought by modern families.

These days, all throughout Japan, ever increasing numbers of condominiums and apartments are being built. These come in a variety of types--usually described as 2DK (2 rooms with a dining room/kitchen), 3DK or 3LDK (3 rooms, a lounge room and dining room/kitchen). Despite having houses furnished in a Western-style, there are many families who seem to favour having a single Japanese-style room, as well. It is not unusual to find condominiums with a Japanese-style room, replete with **tokonoma**--a compromise between Japanese and Western styles, perhaps.

People who live in buildings which are completely airtight and which, naturally, come with efficient air conditioning and heating, are gradually becoming insensitive to the changes of the seasons. Living in a Japanese house, there are frequent opportunities to chat with the neighbours--while hanging out the washing, while doing the gardening and so on, whereas when living in an apartment, there are relatively few occasions when one can meet the people next door. The influences that changing styles of housing have on human society are truly great.

One cannot change houses as if one were simply changing one's clothes. Once a house has been built, our lives are influenced greatly by the environment we live in and by the very construction of the house, itself. As growing numbers of people choose to live in standardized apartments, one cannot help but wonder about what further changes await Japanese society in the future.

◀コースでよいスコアを出すために
練習場でトレーニング。いい感じ
で球がとぶようになると楽しい

見るスポーツで人気が▶
あるのはプロ野球。夏
になるとテレビのナイ
ター中継がはじまる

▼ゲートボールはお年
寄りに人気が高く健
康的なスポーツだ

Ｊリーグの結成でサッカー人気も▶
急上昇。競技場にはたくさんのフ
ァンがつめかける

囲碁(碁)・将棋は中国から伝わったゲーム。囲碁は盤の上に交互に黒と白の石をおいていき、盤上を広く占めたほうが勝ちになる

将棋は並べた20ずつの駒をたがいに動かして、相手の王将をとったほうが勝ちになる

パチンコ人口3,000万人ともいわれ、全国どこの町へ行っても、パチンコ店からチーン、ジャラジャラという玉の出る音が聞こえてくる

カラオケはストレス解消にもってこい。海外にも普及し、国際的な娯楽になった

布で作られたアートフラワー。本物の花にも負けない芸術作品

特別

# 社会人の生活

▲社会人は1日の大半の時間を会社で働いて過ごす。オフィスの中もOA化がすすんでいる

▼通勤ラッシュ。毎朝、駅のホームでくり広げられる光景

▲高度な情報通信機能を備えたオフィスビル（インテリジェントビル）が増えてきた

▼リクルートルックの新入社員たち

# アフター5

仲間と連れだって行きつけの飲み
屋で一杯。残業の疲れをいやす

仕事のあと、帰宅の途中で、飲み
に行く。居酒屋、スナック、カラ
オケバーなど、店はおそくまであ
いている

女性社員はあまいもの
でおしゃべりのひと時

# ●●● 娯楽 ●●●

「日本人は働き蜂」とよく言われます。確かに、日本人は勤勉でよく働き、中には「仕事が趣味」という人もいます。しかし、誰でも仕事ばかりしているわけではありません。それでは、仕事から解放された時、日本人はどんなことに楽しみを見いだすのでしょうか。

まずゴルフです。サラリーマンにとっては、単に趣味というだけでなく「接待ゴルフ」といって、日曜日に青空の下でゴルフをするのは、趣味と仕事の両方ができて、「一挙両得」のようです。

「時間と暇があれば旅行したい」、大部分の日本人がこう考えているのではないでしょうか。国内ばかりか円高の影響から海外旅行熱も高まるばかりで、休日の駅や空港は大変混雑します。

スポーツ観戦は野球、サッカー、相撲などに人気があります。テレビの番組表を見ると、いかに日本人がこれらが好きかがわかります。広いグランドで繰り広げられるゲームや狭い土俵の上の勝負に熱狂し、一時を過ごすのは、たとえテレビの観戦にしても楽しいものです。

また、お年寄りに人気があるのはゲートボールです。孤独になりがちなお年寄りが一緒にボールを追いかけることで、楽しみを共有できるのは良いことだと思います。

パチンコは、好きな人ときらいな人がはっきり別れます。しかし、どんな町にもパチンコ屋が必ずあり、いつも混んでいることを考えると、日本人の娯楽の中に入れる必要がありそうです。パチンコファンは老若男女を問わないようで、店の中には、さまざまな層の人がゲームを楽しんでいます。

カラオケは世代によって楽しみ方が違います。若者はカラオケボックスで、歌うことを目的に、数時間を過ごします。仲間だけでいられること、何人もで楽しめること、歌っている瞬間は主役でいられることなどから人気があるようです。勤め帰りのサラリーマンが、立ち寄るバーなどにも、カラオケの設備のあるところが大半です。「一杯飲み

## Recreation

Japanese people are often described as 'workaholics'. Certainly, Japanese people are industrious and hard-working but, there are also those who regard their work as a 'hobby'. Nevertheless, nobody can be said to devote one's life solely to work. Well then, when Japanese people are released from their working duties, what kind of recreation do they seek out?

To begin with, there is golf. Office workers don't just play golf as a hobby. There is also what is referred to as **settai gorufu** ('golf for business'), golf played on a Sunday--the sun shining--half for pleasure, half for business, killing two birds with one stone, so to speak.

'If I had the time and freedom I'd like to travel' is perhaps a thought on the minds of most Japanese. It is not just travel within Japan that is increasing in popularity--due to the effects of the strong yen, travel abroad is booming and on holidays, railway stations and airports throng with crowds.

People enjoy watching sports like baseball, soccer and **sumo** wrestling. One only has to consult a television guide to discover just how popular these sports are with the Japanese. Spending a short time getting wildly excited about the events unfolding on a vast playing field or about a wrestling match in a small **sumo** ring, even if watched on television, is quite enjoyable.

Tennis is a sport which is popular with people of all ages. Gateball is also a pastime enjoyed by the elderly, who, being prone to loneliness, enjoy the valuable opportunity of being able to share in the pleasure of chasing after a ball with people of their own age.

People are divided in their opinions about **pachinko**, or Japanese pinball--there are those that like it and those that don't. Nevertheless, when you consider that no town is without a pinball parlour and the fact that the parlours are always crowded, **pachinko** seems to deserve its place as one of the recreations that Japanese people enjoy. Pinball parlours are frequented by fans of various age-groups--all enjoying the game--young and old, men and women alike.

Depending upon the generation, people have different ways of enjoying **karaoke** or 'singing to recorded accompaniment'. Young people spend hours in **karaoke** booths for the purpose of singing. Karaoke has proven to be popular with young people for several reasons: friends are able to get together; **karaoke** can be enjoyed by a number of people and **karaoke** provides the opportunity for the person singing to momentarily occupy the limelight. These days, most bars which office workers call in to on the way home from work, are equipped with **karaoke** sound systems. Enjoying **karaoke** over a drink, people unknown to each other pass the microphone backwards and forwards, greeting

ながら」歌うカラオケは、知らない人どうしがマイクを譲り合い、上手な歌に心からの拍手をし、下手な歌にもお世辞の拍手をする。最近では外国人のために、各国語の曲をそろえたところも出てきました。

レンタル・ビデオショップもあちこちで見かけるようになりました。古今東西の映画が自分の家で、しかもレンタル代は1本300円と、手軽に楽しめます。ビデオショップには名画、アクション、スリラー、ドラマ、ポルノなどジャンル別の映画がずらりと並んでいます。これでは映画館がどんどん無くなっていくのも無理はないという気がします。

日本の市町村にはたいてい「文化講座」があって、地域に住む人たちの親睦の機会を提供しています。プログラムは実に多種多様です。その1例をあげてみましょう。

〔書道〕かな、漢字、写経など。白い紙の上に、筆を運びます。白と黒の美、緊張した一瞬と上手に書けた時の喜びは、なかなか良いものです。

〔絵画、写真〕水彩、油絵、パステル画、風景写真、時々展覧会もあり、みんな一心に作品を仕上げます。「日曜画家」といって、休日には公園などでキャンバスに向かって絵をかく人たちをよく見かけます。

〔囲碁・将棋〕お年寄りの男性が大半ですが、中には女性の姿を見ることもあります。2人で向き合って、数時間をすごす、それは非常に知的なゲームです。

〔生け花、アートフラワー〕日本の伝統的な生け花だけではなく、最近ではアートフラワーも人気があります。洋間には、生け花よりも洋風な花の方が合うからでしょうか。そのほかにも、三味線や琴、民謡、踊りなど日本の伝統芸能も盛んです。

カルチャーセンターは、デパートなどが併設している場合も多く、昼間は主婦や退職した年配の人が、夜は仕事帰りのOLやサラリーマンで、どこも一杯です。「娯楽＋学ぶこと」という意味では、やはり「日本人の勤勉さ」に通じるものがありそうです。

skilful singing with heartfelt applause and less able efforts with 'polite' clapping. Recently there have been establishments appearing which offer a full range of songs in a variety of languages in a bid to cater for the numbers of foreign customers.

Video rental shops are becoming an increasingly familiar sight. People enjoy the convenience of being able to watch movies, old and recent, and from all countries, in their own homes for the modest price of 300 yen. In video shops movies are arranged according to their various categories--classics, action movies, thrillers, dramas and 'adult' movies, among others. With this situation, it is no wonder that people feel that movie theatres are soon to become a thing of the past.

In the cities, towns and villages of Japan there are numerous cultural courses which offer people living in these areas the opportunity of a friendly get-together. There are a large number and variety of courses available. One of such courses is calligraphy, for example.

This may involve the writing of kana and Chinese characters or the hand-copying of sutras. Plying a brush to white paper--there's nothing bettter than the feeling of satisfaction one derives from having successfully created a thing of beauty in black and white--performed in an anxious moment.

Painting and photography are also popular. Occasionally exhibitions are held and everyone is busy putting the finishing touches to their work--watercolours, oil paintings, pastels and landscape photography are all put on display. On holidays, in parks and other places, people known as 'Sunday painters' can be often seen bent over their canvases, busily painting.

Most of those who play the games of go and shogi (similar to chess) are elderly men, although there are some women who play, as well. These games, which require a great deal of intellectual ability, may last for hours, with the players pitting their wits against each other.

Recently, Western-style floral arrangement has been gaining in popularity, more so than traditional flower arrangement. Perhaps this is because Western-style flowers go better in the setting of a Western-style room. Other traditional Japanese performing arts that still enjoy popularity are the shamisen, the koto ('Japanese harp'), singing of traditional folk songs and folk dancing.

There are numerous instances of department stores establishing 'cultural centres'. Whether it be with housewives and retired elderly people in the daytime or with office workers on their way home from work in the evenings, wherever you find such places, they are filled to capacity. The popularity of such centres, which provide a combination of recreation and learning, may be interpreted as a gauge of the 'industriousness' of the Japanese people.

# ●●● 社会人の生活 ●●●

日本は世界で一番の長寿国です。平均寿命は男性が約77歳、女性は84歳です。つい最近まで、会社の定年は55歳が平均でしたが、60歳定年制をとる会社が増えてきました。定年は延びても、出生率の低下などから「社会人」（学校を卒業して社会で働く人）は減りつづけ、65歳以上の高齢者が増えていきます。

21世紀の初めには、人口の25パーセントが高齢者で占められ、社会人の肩に日本の社会を支える責任が重くのしかかってきそうです。

社会人は、1日の時間の大半を働いて過ごします。1日8時間の仕事に加えて残業したり、休日出勤のある場合もあります。高度成長期には、「人手が足りなくて困る」という状況でしたが、1991年の「バブルの崩壊」の後は仕事も少なくなりつつあります。サラリーマンの1年の労働時間は、会社によっても違いますが、2000時間前後です。労働省の調査によると2000年の日本人の労働時間の平均が1892時間ということですから、旧西ドイツの1499時間、フランスの1619時間と比べてもかなり多いと言えます。

それでも「働き過ぎではないか」という反省から、週休2日制をとる企業も増えてきました。労働省の調査によると、全企業の約40パーセントが完全週休2日制をとっているそうです。

ILOは1993年の労働報告の中で、「日本の労働者の4割は過労死する」という資料を紹介しました。貿易摩擦の点からも、1週間の労働時間を40時間ぐらいにして社会人はもっと余暇を楽しむべきでしょう。

今まで日本の経済は、ほとんど男性によって支えられてきました。その背後には「男性は仕事だけすればよい。家庭のことは、妻がすべてする」という考え方があります。しかし女性が職場に進出したことから、男女の役割分担が見直されようとしています。

労働時間が減れば、男性が家庭でも妻と協力しあい、家事も分担することができます。「男は仕事、女は家庭」とい

## Life in the Workplace

Japan, at present, enjoys the highest rate of longevity in the world. The average life span for males is approximately 77 years and for females, 84 years. Until very recently, the average retirement age for company employees was 55, however, the number of companies that have adopted a compulsory retirement age of 60 is increasing. Even with the extension of the retirement age, due to factors such as the declining birth-rate and ever-decreasing numbers of Shakaijin ('high school graduates who have become fully-fledged working members of society'), the number of old people above the age of 65 continues to swell.

By the beginning of the twenty-first century, it is expected that 25 percent of the population will comprise old people. The responsibility of supporting Japanese society will weigh heavily upon the shoulders of society's working members.

Working members of Japanese society spend the greater part of a day at work. Most people work an eight hour day. Added to this, there may be overtime and, in some cases, working during holidays. During Japan's period of rapid economic growth there was the problem of a shortage of manpower, however, since 1991, after the bursting of the so-called 'economic bubble', jobs themselves have been becoming scarcer. The number of hours that an average sallaried worker works in a year is about 2000 hours, given slight variation depending upon the company. According to a survey undertaken by the Ministry of Labour, the average number of working hours of the Japanese in 2000 was found to be 1892 hours, which when compared to those of the former West Germany (1499 hours) and France (1619 hours), appears to be a significantly higher figure.

Nevertheless, there are increasing numbers of corporations that have decided to implement a five-day working week after reflecting upon the fact that perhaps people are working too much. A Labour Ministry report has revealed that, about 40 per cent of all corporations have, in fact, instituted a five-day working week.

A 1993 labour report, issued by the International Labour Organization, stated that '40 per cent of Japanese workers die from overwork'. In the light of the trade friction problem, perhaps it would be better for people to work a forty hour week, to thus enable them to enjoy more leisure time.

The Japanese economy to date has been supported by an almost entirely male workforce. Behind this, is the mind-set that 'Men should be the bread-winners. Women should attend to the home.' However, since women have now moved into the work place, the sharing of male and female roles is being reappraised.

As working hours decrease, men will be able to offer their wives more assistance in the home--housework can be shared. It seems that the idea of 'men being the breadwinners and women looking after the home' is gradually changing.

In Japan, large corporations and government and municipal offices adopt a system of 'employment for life'. This is a system

った考えは少しずつ変わっていくと思われます。

日本の大企業や官公庁は、終身雇用制をとっています。新規大学卒業生を、夏から秋にかけての就職試験で採用し、よほどのことがない限り、定年まで雇う制度です。

ふだんはＴシャツにジーンズでいた大学生が、４年生の春ぐらいから急に背広を着たりスーツを着て会社訪問するのが見られます。リクルートルックに身を固めた若者にとって、入社試験は一生を左右する大きな問題です。

会社の場合は、終身雇用制の中で「愛社精神」が生まれ「企業にのために生きる日本人がつくられる」と言えそうです。また官公庁では「親方日の丸」と言われ、絶対につぶれない日本の政府が雇い主ということで、年を経るにしたがって少しずつ出世していきます。

終身雇用制度のもとでの「年功序列制度」では、いくら能力があっても、20代では管理職になれず、能力のある人には不満な人事がされることもあります。

しかし、最近では、この「日本型システム」ともいえる制度が崩れつつあり、早期退職制度や、専門家を契約社員として採用するなど、日本の会社も変わりつつあります。

大企業や官公庁の給与体系は月給制で、１年に数か月分のボーナスが出ます。例えば、月給が30万円でボーナスが６か月分とすると30×（12＋6）で、年収は540万円となります。日本の企業に就職する時は、月給だけではなく、ボーナスや通勤手当、住宅手当などについても確かめることが必要です。

社会人の生活で一番つらいことは「休暇が取りにくいこと」でしょう。どこの会社でも有給休暇のシステムがありますが、それも１年に２週間ぐらいです。「１か月のんびり過ごしたい」と思ったら、会社をやめるか、定年になるのを待つしかありません。最近は夏休みがだんだん長くなる傾向がありますが、それでも１週間から10日です。これから日本の経済も低成長の時代に入ります。やがて、休暇のとり方にも変化が出てくると思われます。

whereby newly graduated university students are selected through employment examinations carried out from summer through to the autumn and, barring extreme circumstances, employs them until retirement.

University students are seen to undergo a change from the spring of their fourth year of study--the normal dress code of jeans and T-shirts is suddenly replaced by that of suits, as students begin calling on companies for interviews. For young people, dressed in preparation for their job interviews, the taking of examinations to enter firms is a crucial occasion, the outcome of which will influence their futures.

The lifelong employment system in companies engenders a spirit of loyalty to the company and it has even been said that 'Japanese were created to live for the companies'. Similarly, when working in government and municipal offices, there is the expression oyakata hinomaru ('the good old government will look after you'), meaning that the Japanese government is the employer, hence, an absolute sense of security is guaranteed. Consequently, as the years go by, slowly but surely, one makes one's mark in the world.

In the 'seniority system', which originates from the lifelong employment system, a person in one's twenties will be unable to attain a managerial position, irrespective of ability. Thus, people of ability may sometimes feeldiscontented regarding certain personnel decisions.

However, recently, this so-called 'Japanese-style system' has begun to show signs of crumbling. The introduction of early retirement and the employment of contracted specialists and such like, reveal that Japanese companies are undergoing change.

Large corporations and government and municipal offices pay wages on a monthly basis, as well as an annual bonus equivalent to several months' pay. For example, where a person receives a monthly salary of 300,000 yen and a bonus equivalent to six months' salary, the annual income would be 5,400,000 yen $[30 \times (12+6)]$. When seeking employment with a Japanese firm, it is necessary to ascertain whether certain allowances are included, such as bonuses, commuting allowance and housing allowance and to not just concern oneself with how much the monthly salary will be.

Perhaps the hardest thing for workers to accept is the fact that 'it is difficult to take holidays'. All companies offer paid leave to workers, however this only amounts to two weeks' annual leave. For those people who feel that they would like to 'take things easy for a month or so', the only choice is to leave the company or to wait for retirement. There has been a growing tendency, recently, for longer summer holidays, but still, these tend to be from only a week to ten days in length. Japan is about to enter a period of low economic growth. As a result, at some time in the future there may be changes in the way people are able to take holidays.

# 年中行事
## Festivals

日本では春夏秋冬、季節の移り変わりがはっきりしています。その季節に合わせて、米作り、農業が盛んに行われてきました。日本の年中行事は、この四季の変化と農業生活に根ざした信仰につながっているものが多いのです。

In Japan, the seasons are distinct as they change through spring, summer, autumn, and winter. In accord with the seasons, rice cultivation and agriculture has thrived. Many Japanese festivals are connected with the change of seasons and agricultural life, and are based on religious beliefs.

## お正月

１月１日は１年のはじめの日で、元日ともいう。神社やお寺は初もうでの人びとでにぎわう

◀おせち料理。正月用の特別料理で、重箱につめる

▼ぞうに。すまし汁やみそ汁にもちと野菜、鳥肉などを入れる

▲年賀状。新年のあいさつを書いたはがきで、友人や知人におくる

▲お年玉。子どもたちは、親や親しいおとなから袋に入れてお金をもらう

▲たこ。糸をつけ、ひっぱりながら空にあげて遊ぶ

◀かるた取り。読み手の読む内容に合った札を多くとった人が勝ち

# 成人の日

この日、市町村などの自治体では、
成人になった男女を集めて祝福する

成人の日（1月の第2月曜日）は、
20歳になったお祝いに、振りそでを
着た女性で、はなやかだ

# 節分

節分の日の夜、家庭では「鬼は外、
福は内」のかけ声とともに豆をま
く。お寺や神社でも年男、年女が
中心になって豆まきをする

# バレンタインデー

この日は、女性が男性にチョコレ
ートをおくる習慣がある。チョコ
レート売り場は女性客で混みあう

## ひな祭り

3月3日は女の子の幸福を願うお祭り。ひな人形をかざって祝う。最近の住宅事情から、小さなひな人形のセットも売られている

▲ひな流しは、紙で作ったひな人形に過去の悪い霊を移して川に流し、災いをとるという、昔からの行事

## 入学式

▲ 4月になると、いっせいに入学式や入社式が行われる。新入生を前に主な大学関係者が壇上にあがって行われる早稲田大学の入学式

幼稚園の入園式に行く▶
晴れ着姿の母と子

# 年中行事

日本では、季節の変化の中で、特定の行事が秩序正しく毎年くりかえし行われます。

現代の日本社会の年中行事は、古い習慣や制度である民俗的なものと、社会の変化に応じて変わっていく風俗的なものが、仲良くとけ合っているといえます。

ここでは、古くから日本の伝統として伝えられた行事と共に、高度成長期以降とくに盛んになった、バレンタインデーやクリスマスも取り上げることにします。

## ●お正月

1年の初め、正月は年中行事の中でももっとも重要なものです。正月は年の神を迎える行事で、きちんと迎えないと、その年が不幸になってしまうと信じられていました。

家の門には門松をたてたり、床の間に鏡もちをお供えしたり、お正月のためにおせち料理を作ったりするのは、全部その年の神様を迎えるための行事です。

### ■門松

門松は常緑樹の松と生命力の強い竹の組み合わせで、健康で長生きできるようにとの願いからです。最近では、アパートに住む人も増えたため門松をたてる家は少なくなりました。それでも、ホテルやデパート、会社などの玄関には大きな門松がたち、都会も新年らしい装いになります。

### ■おせち料理

昔は、お正月のためにどの家もおせち料理を作りましたが、最近ではデパートの食料品売り場などでも買うことができます。おせち料理は日持ちがするように甘い味付けが多く、若者たちにはあまり人気がありません。食べ物の好みの変化や、冷蔵庫の普及によって、おせち料理はだんだん姿を消す傾向にあるようです。

### ■しめ飾り

悪い神様を追い出すためには、家の中のあちこちに、しめ飾りが飾られます。これは人間に災いをもたらす悪い神

## Festivals

In Japan, as the seasons move through their changes, there are a number of annual events which recur regularly every year.

Of the annual events that occur in modern Japanese society, there may be said to be a blending of ancient customs and institutions which reflect the national character, and those customs which change as society itself changes.

In this section, we will examine the cultural traditions of Japan that have been passed on down through the ages, together with those events which have become particularly popular since Japan experienced its rapid economic growth period, such as Valentine's Day and Christmas.

### New Year

In the Japanese calendar year the beginning of the year or New Year represents the most important event. New Year was an event which celebrated the greeting of the 'kami (spirits) of the new year'. It was believed that if this was not done appropriately, it could mean ill fortune for that year. Decorating the entrance gate with pine branches, (Kadomatsu), offering special rice cakes in the tokonoma ('alcove') and preparing special dishes (osechiryori) for the New Year--all these things serve the function of greeting the kami for the new year.

### Kadomatsu
('Decorative Pine Branches')

The Kadomatsu is made up of a combination of pine, being an evergreen, and bamboo, with its sense of vitality; thus, it is meant to represent a wish for good health and long life. Due to the increasing numbers of people living in apartment buildings, fewer houses these days put up decorative kadomatsu. Still, hotels, department stores and companies place large kadomatsu at their entrances, allowing cities, as well, to maintain a New Year's look.

### Osechiryori
('Special New Year Dishes')

In the past, every Japanese family prepared Osechiryori for the New Year season, but recently it has become possible to buy such dishes at the food counters in department stores. Since oshechiryori uses a lot of sweet seasoning to allow the food to keep, it is not so popular with the younger generation. It seems that, with changing dietary habits and the widespread use of refrigerators, osechiryori is tending to disappear.

### Shimekazari
('A Sacred Straw Festoon')

Shimekazari festoon the insides of houses at New Year to ward off evil spirits. In effect they are a kind of curse--an attempt to prevent evil kami ('spirits')

が入ってこないように、呪いの意味があるのです。現代ではこのしめ飾りは家の中だけでなく、車やオートバイにもつけて、交通事故が起きないようにとお願いします。近代化された生活の象徴である車に、最も伝統的なしめ飾りの組み合わせは、日本人の意識の一端を表しているようです。

## ■初もうで

元旦は神社や寺院に初もうでに行きます。東京の明治神宮や大阪の住吉大社などは、300万人もの人がおとずれます。1月3日までは、企業も官公庁もお休みです。正月は家族が集まるときです。結婚して家を離れた息子や娘が、孫をつれて故郷に帰り、家族そろって初もうでに出かける、こんな風景が日本のあちこちで見られます。

## ■お年玉

お年玉は、神様にささげたお供えのお下がりを分けたのがその始まりです。今では、子どもたちは「お正月はお年玉をもらえる日」として、お年玉で預金口座を開く子どもまでいるほどです。文房具店では「お年玉袋」が売られます。

## ■年賀状

元旦には年賀状が届きます。「年賀特別郵便」の制度は1906年（明治39年）に始まりました。それ以来この制度は戦中・戦後、一時的にストップしましたが、現在まで引き継がれ、40億枚もの年賀状が年始めの数日間に、日本中に配達されます。

版画や挿絵など楽しいものも多く、年賀状はお正月の楽しみの一つです。「年賀状だけの付き合い」などという言葉が表すように、年をとっても小学校時代の友達と年賀状を交わしている人もおおぜいいます。年賀状は、疎遠になっていく人間関係を結ぶ、大切な役目を果たしているのです。

## ■遊び

お正月の遊びとして、今ではだんだん少なくなってきましたが、男の子のたこあげ、女の子の羽根つきがあります。カルタ取りは伝統的な遊びで、今でも行われています。

## ●成人の日

1月第2月曜日は成人の日です。20歳になった若者たち

from entering the house, bringing misfortune to people. These days, not only do people decorate the insides of houses with **shimekazari**, but they attach them to cars and motorbikes, expressing a wish to be free from accidents. The combination of the automobile--a symbol of modern-day life and the **shimekazari**--something truly traditional, offers us a glimpse of the consciousness of the Japanese people.

**Hatsumode**
('The First Visit of the Year to a Shrine or Temple')

On New Year's Day people pay their first visit of the year to a shrine or temple. As many as 3 million people visit places such as Meiji Shrine in Tokyo and Sumiyoshi Grand Shrine in Osaka. Businesses and government and municipal offices remain closed until the third of January. New Year is a time when families get together. Sons and daughters who have married and left home return to their ancestral homes with their children. Family groups making their first pilgrimage of the year to a shrine are a common sight throughout Japan at this time.

**Otoshidama**
('A New Year's Gift of Money')

The custom of **Otoshidama** is said to have originated from the division of offerings to the gods, which had been removed from the altar. These days, New Year is regarded as the time when children receive gifts of money, to such an extent that some children even open savings accounts with the money they receive on this occasion. Special envelopes for **Otoshidama** are sold in stationery stores.

**New Year's Cards**

New Year's Cards arrive on New Year's Day. The 'Special New Year's Mail' system was inaugurated in 1899 (the 39th year of the Meiji Era). This mail system has continued from this time to the present day, with temporary suspensions during and after the Second World War. During the first few days of the New Year period, as many as four billion New Year's cards are delivered throughout Japan.

With many attractive woodblock prints and illustrations, New Year's cards represent an enjoyable aspect of New Year's. As is revealed in the expression, to just have a New Year's card relationship', many people exchange New Year's cards with friends from primary school days, as the years go by. New Year's cards fulfil the important function of drawing together the relationships of those people who are becoming estranged from one another.

**New Year Games**

These days, it is becoming increasingly rare to find children playing games at New Year, however, boys can still be found flying kites, while girls may play battledore and shuttlecock. **Karuta**, a traditional card game is still enjoyed today.

**Coming-of-Age Day**

The second Monday of January is Coming-of-

が盛装して成人式に出席し、選挙権を手にし、大人として認められます。お酒やたばこも正式には20歳からです。日本に来て「着物姿が見たい」と思ったら、お正月と「成人の日」は数少ないチャンスです。20歳になった女性たちが、着物姿で歩いているのが見られます。ほとんどがこの日に初めて着物を着たという女性たちで、美容院は着付けに、おおにぎわいです。

　20歳までは犯罪を犯しても、新聞などでは「少年A」などと書かれますが、20歳からはそういうわけにはいきません。それぞれが大人としての自覚を持つ、それが「成人式」なのです。

## ●節分

　2月3日の立春の前夜は「節分」といって豆まきをします。「鬼は外、福は内」と掛け声をかけて、煎った大豆をまきます。これは春を迎える前に悪いものを追い払い、幸運を招くという意味があります。節分は本来、春夏秋冬の分かれ目にあたる立春、立夏、立秋、立冬を言いました。その中で春の節分だけが、年中行事として残ったのです。

　伝統的な年中行事の中でも子どもに人気のあるのが節分です。どこでもお父さんが鬼のお面をかぶり、子どもたちが鬼に向かって豆をぶつけた記憶があると思います。幼稚園や小学校では節分の頃、図画工作の時間に鬼の面をつくります。

　節分にはわかりやすいメッセージが込められている上にふだんとは違う「家族が一緒に遊ぶ」という要素があり、これが、いつまでも人気のある年中行事の秘密なのかもしれません。各地の神社やお寺でも豆まきが行われます。

## ●バレンタインデー

　2月14日は、女性から好きな人に愛を告白できる日です。日本では女性から男性にチョコレートを贈る日としてデパートのチョコレート売り場は大変な混雑です。

　この1か月後はホワイトデーといって、男性から女性にそのお返しをする日です。

Age Day. Young people who have reached the age of twenty, attend Coming-of-Age ceremonies, dressed in their finest clothes. Having finally earned the right to vote, they are recognized as adults. Twenty is also the age at which young people can officially consume alcohol and cigarettes. For those people who come to Japan with the idea of 'seeing someone in a kimono', New Year's and Coming-of-Age Day offer rare opportunities to be able to do so. On these occasions young ladies, recently turned twenty, may be seen walking round in kimono. Most of these ladies will be wearing kimono for the first time, so beauty parlors are a hive of activity at this time--busy helping the young ladies dress.

When a young person below the age of twenty commits a crime, the offender will be referred to as 'Youth A' in newspaper reports, however, once reaching the age of twenty, this will no longer be the case. The Coming-of-Age ceremony marks the time when all young people are made aware of their attainment of adulthood.

**Setsubun**
('The Day Before the Beginning of Spring')

The third of February, the night before the first day of spring is known as Setsubun, when parched beans are scattered. To cries of 'Out with the devil! In with good fortune!', roasted soy-beans are strewn around. This ritual signifies the driving out of bad luck and the calling in of good luck before the arrival of spring.

Originally, setsubun referred to the turning points of each of the four seasons, namely the first days of spring, summer, autumn and winter, respectively. Of these, it is only setsubun, announcing the beginning of spring, which has been retained as an annual event.

Setsubun is a traditional annual event which remains popular with children. Most people probably retain some memory of their father putting on a demon mask, and the children pelting beans at the 'demon'. At the time of setsubun, demon masks are made during handicraft lessons at kindergartens and primary schools.

Having an easily understood significance and providing a rare chance for the family to enjoy themselves together--perhaps these elements provide the key to help us understand why setsubun maintains its popularity as an annual event. Bean scattering ceremonies are carried out at shrines and temples throughout the country.

**Valentine's Day**

The fourteenth of February is a day when ladies are able to declare their true feelings for someone they like. In Japan, ladies give chocolates to men on this day, leading to pandemonium at confectionery centers in department stores. There is also a custom of giving chocolates to male superiors and colleagues in the workplace, even if such people are not particularly liked. These are referred to as 'obligatory chocolates'. 'White Day', celebrated one month after Valentine's Day is a day when men may reciprocate the affection, in turn.

## ●ひな祭り

　3月3日は「ひな祭り」です。女の子が健康に成長するようにとの願いがこめられています。赤いひな壇にひな人形が飾られます。最上段には内裏びな、次の段に三人官女、3段目は五人ばやし、デパートでは2月から7段も8段もあるひな人形が売り出されますが、これを飾れるだけの広い家はどのくらいあるでしょうか。

　もともとは中国から伝わったひな祭りですが、ひな人形が飾られるようになったのは江戸時代からです。

　3月3日から4日にかけては、「流しびな」といって、おひなさまを川や海に流す風習があります。和歌山県や鳥取県の流しびなは、全国的にも有名です。

　ひな壇は早くから飾り、3月3日がすむと、すぐ片づけます。いつまでも飾っておくと「お嫁に行くのがおくれる」と言われるからです。しかし、女性の生き方が多様化し、「嫁にいくこと」にそれほど価値がおかれなくなった今では、このような言い伝えも無意味になってきたようです。

## ●卒業式・入学式

　3月の20日前後はあちこちで卒業式が行われます。日本では、財政の会計年度も学校も会社も、すべて4月から始まり、3月に終わるのです。幼稚園の卒園式、小・中・高校・大学の卒業生は、4月になればまた新たな人生のスタートがあります。

　4月、満開の桜の下で入園式、入学式、入社式などが行われます。新しいランドセルの小学生、慣れない制服を着た中学生や高校生、新調のスーツ姿の新入社員と日本中はフレッシュマンであふれます。

　卒園式や卒業式、入園式、入学式は平日に行われることもあって、母親が出席することが多く、子どもが何人もいるお母さんにとっては、3月、4月はとても忙しい月です。

　最近では育児や教育に父親も参加するところが増え、こういった日に、父親の姿も見られるようになってきました。

## The Doll's Festival

The Doll's Festival is celebrated on the third of March. This occasion signifies the wish for girls to grow up in good health. Dolls are displayed on a red tiered stand. The Emperor and Empress dolls are displayed on the top-most tier; on the second level are three court ladies and on the third, sit five musician dolls. Department stores display Hina dolls of up to seven and even eight tiers in height, from February, but one wonders how many houses have sufficient space to lay out such displays.

The Doll's Festival originally came to Japan from China. It was not until the Edo Period that people began displaying Hina dolls.

From the third of March through to the fourth, the custom of **Nagashibina** is carried out. This involves setting dolls adrift in rivers and in the sea. Tottori Prefecture, in particular, is well-known throughout Japan for this ritual.

The tiered stand of dolls may be displayed rather early but as soon as the third of March has passed, everything is quickly put away. This is because of the belief that if the Hina dolls are displayed indefinitely, 'one's chances of marriage may be delayed'. However, women's lifestyles are changing and in an age when marriage is losing its traditional value, it appears that this kind of belief is disappearing fast.

## Graduation/School Entrance Ceremonies

Around the twentieth of March, graduation ceremonies are held throughout the country. In Japan all schools and companies finalize their financial accounts at the end of March, hence April marks the beginning of the new financial year. April also announces the start of a new life for all those recently graduated from kindergartens, primary schools, junior and senior high schools and universities.

In April, entrance ceremonies for kindergartens, schools and companies take place, often coinciding with the blooming of the cherry blossoms. The country overflows with people making a fresh start--primary school students with their new satchels strapped to their backs, junior and senior high school students wearing uniforms to which they have yet to become accustomed and new company recruits dressed in their newly made suits.

Mothers with a number of children can find themselves rather busy during March and April, since graduation and entrance ceremonies for kindergartens and schools take place on week days and it is mostly the mothers who attend. Recently, fathers have been taking a more active part in the upbringing and education of their children and so, seeing fathers in attendance on such occasions is becoming a more common occurrence.

## 端午の節句

5月5日は男の子の成長を祝う日。
武者人形（上）をかざり、こいの
ぼりをたてる。千葉県茂原市では
毎年こいのぼり祭りを行っている

## 七夕

このごろは、七夕本来の意味から
はなれて、派手なかざりの七夕祭
りが各地で行われる

## お盆・夏祭り

お盆は先祖の霊をなぐさめる仏教行事。この時期になると、各地で、盆おどり、花火大会、夏祭りなど夏の風物がくり広げられる

「子どもみこし」をかついで喜ぶ子どもたち。

見ても楽しい徳島地方の阿波おどり（下）

祭りの日は、みこしをかついで、神社の境内から町中へくり出す

お盆休み、郷里へ帰る人たちで、鉄道も飛行機も交通機関は大混雑、道路も車でいっぱいになる

多くの学校で運動会を開く。1日
中、子どもたちの歓声がきこえる

## 体育の日

気候がよく、この日は会社その他
の団体でも体育の催しが行われる

## 七五三

晴れ着を着て、千歳あめをもって
記念しゃしんをとる

七五三は子どもの成長を祝う行事。3
歳・5歳の男の子、3歳・7歳の女の
子は親に連れられてお宮まいりをする

# クリスマス

日本のクリスマスは宗教に関係な

く、クリスマスツリーがかざられ

クリスマスケーキを買う人でにぎ

わう。イブの東京・銀座の人出

## 歳末

「除夜の鐘」12月31日の午後12時、
各地のお寺でつく鐘の音を聞きな
がら、新しい年をむかえる

正月用のもちつき。都会では一般に米屋
さんに注文したり、出来たおもちを買う

## ●端午の節句

　5月、新緑の季節です。5月5日はカレンダーの上では「子どもの日」で男女共に祝う日ですが、もともとは「端午の節句」といって、男の子の成長を祝う日でした。新緑の下で「鯉のぼり」が風にはためき、男の子のいる家では「武者人形」が飾られます。菖蒲をお風呂に入れる「菖蒲湯」は、「勝負に強くなるように」という意味が重なっています。

　4月29日が「緑の日」、5月3日は「憲法記念日」5月4日は「国民の休日」ということで、土曜、日曜をつなげるとかなりの休みがとれることから、お正月、お盆について、おとなも子どもも楽しみにしている休日です。この期間はゴールデンウイークと呼ばれ、日本中の行楽地はどこも満員です。

## ●七夕

　7月7日は七夕です。銀河の東西にある牽牛星と織女星が年に一度会うという中国の伝説があります。七夕は、この話と日本古来の風習が重なったものです。

　七夕の歴史は古く、万葉集（日本で一番古い歌集）には100以上もの七夕のうたが詠まれています。

　江戸時代には七夕は5節句（1月7日、3月3日、5月5日、7月7日、9月9日）の一つとして、江戸幕府の公式行事でした。広重の「名所江戸百景」には、江戸の町のあちこちの家々に、笹竹が飾られている様子が描かれています。

　その後、1873年（明治6年）に、公式行事として七夕が廃止されてから、だんだん小規模のお祭りになっていったようです。

　しかし、今でも七夕の前になると、文房具店では短冊が売られ、花屋では笹が売りに出されます。幼稚園や小学校の低学年では、図画や工作の授業の中で、七夕飾りが作られます。竹に「〜がほしい」とか「〜になりたい」といった願い事を書いた短冊を結びつけます。昔は家々の軒先に笹竹が飾られましたが、マンションやアパートに住む人が

## Boys' Festival

May is a time of new green leaves. On the calendar, the fifth of May is marked as 'Children's Day', a celebration dedicated to both boys and girls alike. However, originally, this day was called 'Boys' Festival', a day put aside to celebrate the healthy growth of boys. Against this backdrop of fresh green leaves, carp streamers may be seen fluttering in the breeze, and houses where there are boys in the family will display warrior dolls. Japanese irises, **shobu**, are put into the bath water. This custom is known as **shobu-yu** and signifies a desire for 'strength in contest', the word for 'contest' sharing the same pronunciation as for the word for 'Japanese iris', **shobu**.

April 29th is 'Greenery Day', May 3rd is 'Constitution Memorial Day' and May 4th is designated a 'National Holiday'. When these holidays are coupled with Saturday and Sunday, it amounts to a reasonably long holiday break. Consequently, adults and children alike, look forward to these holidays, as they do New Year's and the **Bon** Festival holidays. The period from April 29th to May 5th is known as 'Golden Week', during which time resort areas throughout Japan are full to capacity.

## Tanabata ('The Star Festival')

**Tanabata** is celebrated on the 7th of July. According to Chinese legend, the Cowherd Star (Altair) and the Weaver Star (Vega) come from opposite eastern and western extremes of the Milky Way once a year, to meet. Tanabata, as it is known today has its origins in this legend and ancient Japanese tradition.

**Tanabata** has a long history and in fact, more than one hundred poems from the Manyoshu (Japan's oldest anthology of poems) were composed for 'The Star Festival'.

During the Edo Period, **Tanabata** was one of the five official festivals (January 17th, March 3rd, May 5th, July 7th and September 9th) and was recognized as a state function of the Edo Shogunate. In the painter Hiroshige's work '100 Views of Edo', houses throughout the city of Edo are seen decorated with bamboo and bamboo grass, characteristic of this festival time.

Later, in 1873 (the 6th year of the Meiji Era), **Tanabata** was abolished as a state event and over the years, has become a festival of a much smaller scale.

Even these days, shortly before the **Tanabata** festival, stationery stores do a brisk trade in fancy paper for writing traditional poems and florists display bamboo grass for sale. Lower classes in kindergartens and primary schools make **Tanabata** decorations in their drawing and craft classes. Fancy strips of paper are tied to bamboo which have wishes such as 'I would like 〜' or 'I want to be 〜' written on them. Formerly, houses displayed bamboo grass at the eaves, but for urban dwellers, mostly living in apartments, it is as much as they can do to display the bamboo on the balcony.

Sendai and Hiratsuka are renowned for their **Tanabata** festivals. The decorations in the covered shopping malls in these

多い都会では、ベランダに飾るのが精一杯です。

仙台や平塚の七夕は有名で、商店街の飾りは年々豪華になってきています。もともとは陰暦の7月7日に行われたもので、今でも1月遅れで祝う地方が多いようです。

7月から8月にかけては、お祭りが多く、福岡の博多山笠、京都の祇園祭、大阪の天神祭、青森のねぶたまつりなど、有名なお祭りがつづきます。また、夏の風物として各地で花火大会が開かれますが、とくに東京の隅田川の花火は有名です。

## ●お盆

8月の15日前後はお盆で、仏教行事と、亡くなった先祖を迎えて生活の繁栄を願うという日本独特の風習が重なったものです。

お盆に実家に帰省してお墓まいりをする人もたくさんいます。お寺や霊園の駐車場はどこも満員で、お墓まいりで久しぶりに親戚と顔を合わせたり、お墓に花を飾ったり、先祖のために供養する時です。

この時期に「お盆休み」をとる会社が多く、鉄道も飛行機も、郷里へ帰る家族たちでにぎわいます。各地では盆踊りが行われ、浴衣姿の人びとが中央にたてられた櫓のまわりで、輪になって踊ります。最近では都会の団地などでも盆踊りが行われるようになりました。地域の共同体の意識を高めるという意味でも意義深い夏の催しです。

## ●お月見 （中秋の名月、9月15日頃）

日本は昔、月の満ち欠けによって月日を数える太陰暦を使っていました。1日は新月、15日は満月です。現在では太陽暦を使っているために毎年お月見の日が違ってきます。

旧暦の8月15日に満月を眺めるのは、平安時代に中国の唐から伝わったとされています。日本でも万葉集の時代から、月が満ちたり欠けたりするのは、復活と不死の象徴とされていました。また十五夜が特別の意味を持っていたのは、『竹取り物語』で「かぐや姫」が十五夜の夜に月の世界に帰るというストーリーからも知ることができます。

cities seem to grow more and more elaborate as the years go by. Since **Tanabata** was formerly held on the 7th day of the 7th month of the Lunar Calendar, there are still many regions today that celebrate this event one month after the 7th of July.

**Obon** ('The Lantern Festival')

The **Bon** Festival, celebrated around the 15th of August is a combination of Buddhist tradition and the unique Japanese custom of greeting the spirits of deceased ancestors in the hope of leading a prosperous life.

From July to August numerous well-known **omatsuri** or festivals are held throughout the country, including Fukuoka's **Hakata Yamagasa**, Kyoto's **Gion Matsuri**, Osaka's **Tenjin Matsuri** and Aomori's **Nebuta Matsuri**. Fireworks displays, very mach a part of summer, take place at this time, as well. The display of fireworks on the Sumida River in Tokyo is particularly renowned.

At the time of **Obon** many people return to their parental homes and visit ancestral graves. On this occasion memorial services are held in honour of the ancestors. Car parks for temples and cemeteries are filled to overflowing as people who have come to visit graves meet relatives they have not seen for some time and place floral tributes.

As many companies take **Obon** holidays at this time of year, trains and planes are full of families returning to their hometowns. **Bon** Festival dances are performed throughout the country with people wearing summer **kimono**. They form a ring and dance around a high wooden stage which has been specially erected. In recent times, **Bon** dances have begun to be held in housing complexes in the cities, as well. Since such dances serve to strengthen the sense of communal spirit throughout the various regions, they represent a significant summer entertainment.

**Moon-Viewing** ('The Harvest Moon', around the 15th of September)

Japan formerly employed the lunar calendar, counting the days and months, according to the waxing and waning of the moon. The first of the month was the new moon while the 15th of the month corresponded to the full moon. Since the solar calendar is now used, the date on which moon viewing is carried out changes each year.

It is believed that the custom of viewing the full moon on the 15th day of the 8th month of the old lunar calendar came to Japan from the Tang Dynasty of China at the time of the Heian Period. Even in Japan, from the time of the **Manyoshu**, the waxing and waning of the moon is said to have symbolized rebirth and immortality. A further reason that the night of the 15th retains a special significance is that in the story **Taketori Monogatari** ('The Tale of the Bamboo Cutter'), Princess Kaguya-hime is said to have returned to the realm of the moon on the night of the 15th day of the month.

## ●体育の日

10月の第2月曜日は体育の日で、日本中の学校のあちこちで運動会や体育大会が行われます。1964年に行われた東京オリンピックを記念して作られた祭日です。しかし、その日は子どもが騎馬戦やかけっこをするのを見ようと、父母がお弁当を持って駆けつけたり、他校の生徒が見学に来たりと、子どもにとっては特別な日になっています。

## ●七五三

11月15日、3歳、7歳の女の子、3歳、5歳の男の子が両親に連れられて、神社にお宮まいりをします。3歳の女の子は着物の上に赤い被布（コート）を着ます。7歳の女の子は着物、男の子はブレザー姿が多いようです。神社では神主さんが、健康に成長するようにと御祓いをします。

七五三は宗教に関係なく、お宮まいりをする家庭が一般的です。

3歳、7歳の女の子は昔は着物を着ていましたから「帯の祝い」といって、つけひもをとって帯をし始める日でした。また男の子は袴を着るお祝いでもありました。

七五三という名称が使われはじめたのは明治以後で、東京から関西に広まり、今では全国的に行われています。

## ●クリスマス

キリスト教の国のクリスマスと違い、日本のクリスマスには、ほとんど宗教的な意味がありません。クリスマスは、クリスマスツリーとクリスマスプレゼント、そしてローソクとクリスマスケーキのある、家族や友人が集まるパーティーになっているのです。

日本では、お正月についでクリスマスをしている家庭が多く、サンタクロースの存在を信じている子どもも少なくありません。キリスト降誕の12月25日は、日本では家族だんらんの日として定着しているようです。

### Health-Sports Day

The second Monday of October is Health-Sports Day and schools throughout Japan hold field days and athletic carnivals on this day. This national holiday was created to commemorate the Tokyo Olympic Games which took place in 1964. These occasions are special times for children--mothers, with prepared packed lunches flock to see their young ones taking part in mock cavalry battles and footraces, while students visit from other schools to spectate.

### Shichi-Go-San
(literally 'seven-five-three')

On the 15th of November, girls of 3 and 7 years of age and boys of 5 years of age visit their tutelary shrines, accompanied by their parents. Three-year-old girls wear a special red coat over their kimono. Seven-year-old girls wear kimono and boys mostly wear jackets these days. At shrines, Shinto priests carry out purification rites to ensure the healthy growth of the children. (Shinto Priests are given anywhere from a few thousand yen to tens of thousands of yen as payment for such services.) It is usual for families to pay a visit to shrines at the time of Shichi-go-san, regardless of religious persuasion.

In the past, this occasion was known as the 'Obi Festival', since it was the day when three and seven-year-old girls would wear their kimono with a proper obi or sash, having removed the cord they formerly wore, for the first time. It was also a celebration when boys wore hakama (a divided skirt-like garment).

The name Shichi-go-san began to be used after the Meiji Period; its popularity spread from Tokyo to the Kansai area and today, this event is celebrated on a national scale.

### Christmas

Christmas in Japan differs from Christmas as celebrated in Christian countries and has little religious significance. To Japanese, Christmas signifies a time of Christmas trees and presents, of candles and Christmas --an occasion when family and friends get together for parties.

In Japan, may families celebrate Christmas, just as they do New Year and quite a lot of children believe in Santa Claus.

December 25th, a celebration of the birth of Christ, in Japan seems to have become established as a day for the gathering of happy family groups.

## ●歳末

12月28日は官公庁の「仕事納め」の日です。12月29日から大晦日までの休日は、日本の家庭では大掃除をしたり、お正月の準備をしたり、大忙しです。

元旦に食べるおぞうにのもちや、鏡もちは最近ではお米屋さんに注文すると配達してくれます。最近のおもちは真空パックになっていて日持ちし、またいつでも買えることから、お正月の御馳走としての価値は薄れつつあります。

地方では今でもお正月の準備に「もちつき」をするところがあります。家族や親戚が集まって、臼と杵でもち米をペッタンペッタンとつき、できたてのもちを食べます。これは一種のイベントとして引き継がれていきそうです。

年末の掃除は「大掃除」といって、特に念を入れて掃除をします。窓をふいたり、床を磨いたり、引き出しを整理したり、障子やふすまを張り替えたりします。多くの家では男性が手伝うことが多く、ここにも「大掃除」が一家が団結して行う1つの行事としての意味があるようです。

12月31日は「大晦日」です。大掃除もすみ、お正月を迎える準備ができた部屋で「年越しそば」を食べます。午後12時になると「除夜の鐘」が鳴ります。

近くに寺院があるところでは、冬の澄んだ空気の中を、除夜の鐘の「ゴーン、ゴーン」という音がひびきわたり、本当にいいものです。

年越しそばを食べる習慣は、江戸時代の中期に始まりました。そばは細く長いので長寿に通じ、また簡単に切れることから病気や借金と「縁が切れる」ということです。

年越しそばを食べおわり、夜中の12時を過ぎるとお正月です。「明けましておめでとう」と家族で挨拶します。

その後は寒い中を元気良く初もうでに出かける人もいます。大晦日の電車や地下鉄は、特に終夜運転をして初もうで客のためにサービスしてくれます。

年中行事はもともと宗教を起源に持つものでしたが、キリスト教には関係ないクリスマス、神道でなくても初もうでに出かけるというように世俗化してきていると言えます。

## The Year-End

December 28th is the last official working day of the year for government and municipal offices. There is great activity in Japanese households during the holidays from the 29th of December to New Year's Eve, as families carry out a thorough house-cleaning and get ready for New Year's.

In recent years it has become possible to have home delivery of rice cakes for ozoni, a kind of soup which is eaten on New Year's Day and kagami-mochi, special mirror-shaped rice cakes for offerings, by ordering them from rice dealers. These days the status of rice cakes as New Year delicacies is declining due to increased availability and since vacuum-sealed packaging allows them to keep well.

In regional areas, mochitsuki or 'rice cake making' is still carried out today, as part of the preparations for New Year. Family members and relatives get together, and after pounding glutinous rice using a mortar and a wooden pestle, they eat the freshly made rice cakes together. As a kind of special 'event', this custom seems destined to continue for some time.

The house-cleaning which is carried out at the end of the year is particularly thorough and is known as osoji ('general house-cleaning'). Windows are cleaned, floors are polished, drawers are tidied and sliding doors are re-papered. In many households, men assist with the cleaning and for this reason, osoji is significant in that it represents one of the events carried out by the family working as one body.

The evening of December 31st is omiso-ka ('New Year's Eve'). Once the general house-cleaning has been carried out, the family eat toshi-koshi soba, a special kind of buckwheat noodles, in a room which has been prepared to see the New Year in. At the stroke of midnight, the temple bells begin to ring in the New Year. To hear the slow chiming of the temple bells resonating through the crisp, clear winter air, at a nearby temple, is truly a remarkable experience.

The custom of eating buckwheat noodles at New Year began around the middle of the Edo Period. The noodles, being long and thin are thought to represent long life and the fact that the noodles are easily cut is meant to signify a quick release from illness and debt.

Once the toshikoshi noodles have been eaten and it is past midnight, it is officially New Year's. Family members then greet each other with the phrase Akemashite omedeto ('A Happy New Year to You!').

After this ritual has taken place, there are some people who set out to pay their first visit of the year to the local shrine, bracing themselves against the cold. On New Year's Eve, the railways and subways run special services throughout the night to cater for people making their first pilgrimage of the year.

The Annual Events of Japan have origins bearing religious significance, however, it would seem that these events have adapted to the 'masses', giving rise to phenomena such as a Christmas which has little to do with Christianity, and people making their first visit of the year to the local shrine, regardless of being Shintoist, or not.

# 日本の文化
## Japanese Culture

文化には、むかしからある伝統文化として、歌舞伎、能・狂言などの演劇や茶道、華道、書道などの芸術があります。また、現代の文学、音楽、美術、映画などの現代文化、子どもの世界に特有の子ども文化があります。

Within the area of culture, there is the traditional culture passed down through history, for example the performing arts of Kabuki, Noh, and Kyogen, as well as the fine arts of tea, flower arranging and calligraphy, Then, there is also contemporary culture, with moderm literature, music, art, and movies, as well as a unique culture in the world of children.

# ●●● 伝統文化 ●●●

和室の床の間には、掛け軸をかけ花を飾る

客を招いてお茶をたてて出す茶の湯（茶道）。切り花を花器に飾って眺める生け花（華道）。今も普及している伝統文化に退社後や休日、教室に通う人が多い

歌舞伎は、外国人に一番よく知られた伝統芸能。舞台も着物もはなやかで美しい。後ろで三味線・つづみなど伴奏音楽を演奏している

# 歌舞伎

歌舞伎舞踊「藤娘」の舞台。藤の枝をもって踊る女形（男の役者）

歌舞伎代表劇の一つ「暫」。顔のくまどりに迫力がある

46

能は古くから伝わる歌舞劇。能面
をつけたシテ方（主役）とワキ方
（脇役）、おはやし方で演じる

# 能と狂言

狂言は能と能の間に同じ舞台で演
じられる喜劇。音楽はなく、セリ
フと動作のおもしろさで笑わせる

筆と墨で文字を書く書道は、中国から伝わったが、日本でかな文字が加わり、独自の芸術として発達した

筆の勢い、文字のバランス、墨の濃淡など、上手になるための練習をつづける

琴は日本音楽（邦楽）の代表的な楽器。三味線・笛など、ほかの楽器との合奏、琴による西洋音楽の演奏もある

## 日本の文化

Japanese Culture

### ●●● 伝統文化 ●●●

　1960年代の高度成長によって、日本の社会は急速に近代化しました。それ以前に日本をおとずれたことのある外国人は日本的なものが姿を消してしまっていることに、がっかりするようです。

　しかし、高速道路が都市をつなぎ、高層ビルが立ち並ぶ都会にも、まだ日本的な伝統文化は引きつがれています。

　高層ホテルのロビーには生け花が飾られているし、和室に通されると、床の間には掛け軸がかけられています。

　スマートなスーツ姿のＯＬが、会社の帰りに茶の湯教室に通ったり、歌舞伎を見たり、いくら生活が近代化しても日本の伝統文化は生きつづけているのです。

　最近はワープロで手紙を書く人が多くなりました。しかし「お正月くらいは、年賀状を筆で書きたい」という人も多いのです。

### ●歌舞伎

　歌舞伎は日本の伝統芸能の中でも一番人気が高いものです。東京には歌舞伎座と国立劇場がありますが、人気のある出し物の時には、良い席はなかなかとれないほどです。

　歌舞伎の特徴は何といっても、演じる人がすべて男性だということです。「女形」といって女の役を演じる役者がいます。その物腰は女よりも女らしく、作りごと（フィクション）の世界で理想の女性像を演じているといえます。

　舞台の左側には、歌舞伎の伴奏音楽をする下座があり、三味線や長唄が演奏されています。

　舞台は回り舞台で、観客席から見ていると、舞台が右から左に役者をのせたまま動いていき、すばやく次の場面に変わります。いちいち幕を閉めたり開けたりする必要がなく役者が舞台と一緒に登場したり退場したりするのは、見ていても面白いものです。

## Japanese Culture

### Traditional Culture

During the 1980's, when Japan experienced a high level of economic growth, Japanese society underwent rapid modernization. It would seem that foreigners who visited Japan prior to this time have expressed disappointment at the fact that certain 'Japanese things' have vanished without a trace.

Nevertheless, cities today may be linked by motorways--skyscrapers may dot the skyline of such cities and yet, examples of uniquely Japanese traditional culture continue to be found.

The lobbies of multi-storied luxury hotels are decorated with **ikebana** or 'arranged flowers'. When one is shown into a Japanese room, hanging scrolls displayed in the alcove area are to be observed.

Office girls, wearing elegant Western-style suits attending tea ceremony classes on the way home from the company, or going to see a **Kabuki** performance--evidence of Japan's thriving traditional culture, no matter how modern the lifestyle one chooses to lead.

In recent times, increasing numbers of people are using word processors for letter writing. However, there are quite a few people who feel that they would like to write their New Year's cards, at least, with brush and ink.

### Kabuki

**Kabuki** is the most popular of the traditional Japanese theatrical arts. Tokyo is the home of the **Kabuki-za** Theatre and the National Theatre. Certain Kabuki programmes at these theatres can prove to be so popular that good seats can be hard to obtain.

The characteristic that undeniably sets Kabuki apart from other forms of theatre, is the fact that all roles are performed by men. There are actors who specialize in the performance of female roles, known as **onnagata**. The manner of such actors appears to be more feminine than that of women and it is said that, in this make-believe world, they capture the ideal image of womanhood in their acting.

To the left of the stage is the musician's box, occupied by the **shamisen** players and **nagauta** ('a long epic song') performers. These people provide the musical accompaniment for Kabuki.

The Kabuki stage is a revolving stage with the actors on stage moving from right to left--one scene quickly changes to another, as the audience watches. It is is a fascinating experience to watch the actors

また花道といって、舞台から直角に観客席に突き出した形で道が伸びています。花道は役者の登場・退場だけではなく舞台の一部として川や家の廊下になったりするのです。

歌舞伎のセリフは日本人にもわかりにくく、イヤホーンガイドが歴史的な背景やセリフの現代語訳などを、解説してくれます。英語の説明もあります。そうすれば、単に舞台を見てわからないストーリーを追っているよりは、ずっと理解が深まるでしょう。

歌舞伎は様式美の世界です。感情が最高潮に達した時、役者が行動を停止し、まるで舞台が「絵」のような状態になります。役者が見得をきると、観客を含めた劇場全体が静止したような状態になります。その静止を破るかのように「いよー、はりまや」などと観客席から掛け声がかかり拍手が起きます。これこそが歌舞伎の見せ場とも言えるものです。

そのほかにも、歌舞伎の見所はたくさんあります。役者のくまどりや着物、音楽などです。約400年の伝統の上にたつ歌舞伎は、これからもさまざまな工夫を加えながら後世に引きつがれていくでしょう。

## ●茶道

茶道は戦国時代に千利休（1522−91）によって完成されたものです。「お茶を入れる」ということは、日頃戦いに明け暮れる武士だからこそ必要な、静かに過ごす時間だったのでしょう。それ以来、茶道は日本人の礼儀作法の１つとして受けつがれてきました。

今でも、茶道を習う人は多く、カルチャースクールなどには必ずといってよいほど「茶道教室」があります。ただし、お茶をたてるには、茶室と言われる特別の畳の部屋や道具が必要で、日本人の日常生活の中から、茶道はだんだん姿を消す運命にあるようです。

## ●生け花

生け花は「華道」とも言われます。それは外観の装飾性よりも「花を通じて自己を表現する」精神性を重んじてい

---

appear and disappear as the stage rotates, there being no necessity to open and close the curtain at the change of each scene.

There is also a walkway which juts out into the audience at right angles to the stage, known as the **hanamichi**. The **hanamichi** is not only used for the arrival and departure of the actors, but actually becomes part of the stage and may serve as a river or a corridor in a house, for example.

Since the dialogue used in Kabuki is difficult even for Japanese people to understand, an 'ear-phone guide' service is provided, explaining the historical background of the play and giving a modern Japanese translation of what is being said. English versions are also available. In this way, the audience may gain a much deeper insight rather than just staring at the stage trying to follow a seemingly incomprehensible story.

The world of Kabuki is one of the beauty of style. At particular times of emotional climax, the actors freeze and the stage takes on a picture-like quality. A hush falls over the whole theatre, including the audience, as the actors assume their flamboyant poses. At this time, shattering the silence, members of the audience shout out words of encouragement, such as **iyo** and **harimaya**, whereupon the scene is greeted with applause. Such moments are the highlights of Kabuki performances.

Kabuki has many other interesting aspects--the actors' make-up, costumes and the music--to name but a few. With its four hundred years of tradition, and by adding to its many and varied devices, perhaps Kabuki will continue to entertain future generations.

**Sado** (Tea Ceremony)

The Tea Ceremony was perfected by **Sen-no-Rikyuu** (1522-1591) during the age of civil wars. For warriors who were perpetually at battle, day in day out, the art of making tea perhaps provided just the quiet time of relaxation needed. The tea ceremony has been inherited from this time as an example of Japanese etiquette.

Even today, many people learn the tea ceremony and cultural centres, almost without fail, offer tea ceremony classes. However, since a **chashitsu** ('tea ceremony room')--a special room with **tatami** mats and implements, is needed for the making of tea, it seems that the tea ceremony is destined to disappear from the everyday lives of Japanese people.

**Ikebana** (Flower Arrangement)

Ikebana is also known as **kado** ('the way of the flower'). In this traditional art, there is a greater value placed on 'spirituality' and the expression of self through flowers, rather than on an outward show of ostentation.

There are many different schools of

るからでしょう。

　生け花にはさまざまな流派があり、それぞれに先生を頂点とし、門弟がその下にピラミッドのようにつらなる家元制度と呼ばれる組織があります。しかし、どの流派にも共通することは「生け花は生きている草木を材料にした瞬間的な芸術」ということです。ここにも、俳句をよむ時とあい通じる「瞬間」を大切する心が生きています。

## ●短歌と俳句

　短歌は5・7・5・7・7の5句、31音を定型とする歌です。ふつう和歌というと短歌をさします。現代では自然な話し言葉による口語短歌もさかんです。

　「この味がいいね」と　君が言ったから　7月6日はサラダ記念日　（俵万智）

　俳句は短歌の初めの5・7・5の部分をとったもので、世界で一番短い定型詩と言えるのではないでしょうか。
　「静けさや　岩にしみいる　蟬の声」これは有名な芭蕉の俳句です。俳句には季語が含まれていることが条件です。この場合は「蟬」が季語で夏を表します。使われる音数が17音であることも条件ですが、最近の現代俳句には季語もなく、音数にこだわらないものも出ています。
　「ほかでもない　生きるということは　選ぶということ」

　　　　　　　　　　　　　　　　　　　　瓜生敏一

　こうなると、俳句の感じもだいぶ違ってきますね。

## ●書道

　書道は中国から伝わった漢字で書かれた「お経」を写すことから始まりました。そして平安時代に仮名が発明されると、中国とは趣の違う仮名書道が発達しました。
　まだ学校制度のなかったころから、書道は算盤と共に子どもたちの教育の中心になるものとして習われてきました。寺子屋が学校のかわりをしていたのです。江戸時代には武士階級ばかりではなく、庶民階級でも識字率が高かったことが記録に残っています。
　現在、日本の学校では「国語」の時間に書道を取り入れ

Ikebana. Each of these is a pyramid-like organization, with a grand-master at the apex and followers filling up the lower ranks. This kind of organization is referred to as the *iemoto* ('head master') system. Though there be many different schools, they all share a common belief in the art of *Ikebana*--that of 'capturing a moment', using living trees and plants as raw materials.

Here, too, the spirit which values the 'moment' lives, related to the spirit in which one composes haiku poetry.

### Tanka and Haiku

Tanka is a fixed five-line form of Japanese verse consisting of 31 syllables (a 5. 7. 5. 7. 7 arrangement). In Japanese, when you talk of **waka** ('a Japanese poem'), you are normally referring to **tanka**. These days colloqual -style **tanka**, which employ natural spoken language, are popular. Note Machi Tawara's example: '"Tastes great" you told me, And so, the 6th of July – Our salad anniversary'

Haiku derive from the first three lines of the **tanka** verse form and might be described as the world's shortest fixed-verse form. An example from Basho, the famous haiku poet: 'Silence – Into the very rocks it seeps – The cicada cry'
One of the conditions of writing a **haiku** is that it must contain a reference to the seasons. In Basho's poem, 'cicada' is the season word, which evokes 'summer'. Limiting the length to 17 syllables is a further condition of **haiku** writing. However, in modern haiku poetry, there are poems that contain no seasonal reference and no strict adherence to the set number of syllables.
Here is such an example: "Living Is about choosing – Nothing else"
(Toshikazu Uryuu)
This style of modern verse presents **haiku** in a radically different light.

### Calligraphy

The art of calligraphy originates from China where there was a practice of copying Buddhist sutras which were written in Chinese characters. Then, in the Heian Period, with the invention of **kana**, or the indigenous Japanese syllabary, **kana** calligraphy, quite unlike its Chinese equivalent, developed.

At a time when there was no formal system of schools, children learned calligraphy and the use of the abacus, these skills constituting the priority of education at this time. Private schools run by temples took the place of state schools. Records remain today that show that during the Edo Period, there was a high level of literacy among the common people and not just among the **samurai** class.

At present, in Japanese schools, calligraphy is part of the Japanese language syllabus and so, the majority of Japanese peo-

ているので、大部分の日本人は筆を持ち、半紙に向かって「緊張した時」を過ごした経験をしています。

## ●能と狂言

能は「能楽」ともいって、日本の代表的舞台芸術の１つで、約700年の伝統があります。奈良時代に、中国の唐から大衆芸能として伝わった「能楽」が、鎌倉時代に唄や舞踏劇の「能」と対話劇の「狂言」へとわかれました。

室町時代になると、観阿弥、世阿弥の親子が能を芸術的なものへと発展させ、現在まで受け継がれています。

能は「能楽堂」と呼ばれる、屋根のある特別な舞台で上演されます。

能は主役のシテ方（たいてい面をつける）、ワキ方（面をつけない人）、とおはやし方（笛や太鼓の楽器を演奏する人）によって演じられます。

舞台装置は何もありません。ストーリーの流れの中から大きな山や海、強い風などを想像するのです。かえって何もないことで、私たちの想像力は無限にふくらんでいくのです。

能と狂言は一番ずつ交互に上演されます。能のまじめなストーリーを緊張して見た後は、くつろいだ気持ちで狂言を楽しみます。セリフが面白いばかりでなく、動作もユーモラスで、観客もつい笑いの世界にひきこまれます。

能と狂言が交互にあるのは、なかなか考えた演出だと思います。

## ●日本の音楽

明治時代に日本に入ってきた西欧の音楽を「洋楽」と言うのに対して、昔から伝えられた日本の音楽を「邦楽」と言います。雅楽、能楽、俗曲などです。

邦楽の特徴は洋楽の音階が７つあるのに対して５音階であること、洋楽のリズムは一拍の長さが同じであるのに、邦楽は長さが一定でないことなどです。最近では和楽器の代表ともいえる琴でバロック音楽を演奏するなど、音楽も今までとは違う楽しみ方が生まれています。

ple have had the experience of that 'tense moment'--brush in hand and a piece of rice paper before them.

### Noh and Kyogen

Noh, also known as Nogaku, is one of Japan's typical theatrical arts and has a history dating back approximately seven hundred years.

Nogaku came to Japan during the Nara Period from the Tang Dynasty in China where it was a form of public entertainment. Later, in the Kamakura Period, it was divided into Noh, a combination of singing and dance drama, and Kyogen, a dialogic play.

In the Muromachi Period, Kan Ami and Ze Ami, father and son, developed Noh to an art form, which has been handed down to the present day.

Noh is performed on a special stage known as a Nogaku-do, which has a canopy.

In Noh, the performers consist of the leading actor (usually wearing a mask), the supporting actors (without masks) and the musical accompanists (playing flute and drums).

There are no stage settings in Noh performances. Tall mountains, the sea, strong winds--elements which may arise as the story unfolds, are imagined by the audience. Since there is nothing to be seen, this adds to the potential of the limitless scope of the imagination.

A Noh performance is always followed by a Kyogen performance. After watching a serious Noh play in a somewhat tense atmosphere, one can enjoy the relaxed mood of the Kyogen play. It is not just a question of the dialogue being humorous--the action is comic and before one realizes it, one finds onself laughing.

Noh and Kyogen being performed in tandem, one after the other, is certainly a well thought-out dramatic presentation.

### Japanese Music

Western music which was introduced into Japan during the Meiji Period is known as Yogaku ('western music'), while that which has come down through the generations in Japan is referrred to as Hogaku ('traditional Japanese music') and includes Gagaku ('Imperial court music'), Nogaku ('Noh play music') and folk balads.

Traditional Japanese music is distinctive in that, unlike western music with its 7-note scale, hogaku has a pentatonic scale and, while in Western music, the length of each beat is the same, there is no such uniformity in traditional Japanese music. Recently there have been arrangements made in Baroque Music for the Koto ('Japanese harp'), a typical traditional Japanese instrument, evidence that different ways of enjoying music are emerging.

# ●●● 現代文化 ●●●

川端康成。1968年、ノーベル文学
賞を受ける。代表作「雪国」執筆
の頃の著者

大江健三郎。1994年ノーベル文学
賞受賞。記念講演「あいまいな日
本の私」を収めた本と代表的作品

1994年完成の「江戸東京博物館」。
最新の建物の中に江戸時代を再現
している。上は昔の日本橋風景

美術館「大倉集古館」には近代日本画の代表的作品や東洋陶器の名品が数多く集められている。
近代から現代にかけての代表的日本画家、横山大観の「夜桜屏風」。

音響効果のすぐれた新しいホール、東京芸術劇場（左）やサントリーホール（右）では、世界の有名音楽家や楽団の演奏が行われる

映画館のお客は減ったが、人気の映画がある時はやはり混雑する

ＣＤ.ビデオレンタルは若者を中心に利用者が増えている

54

# ●●● 子ども文化 ●●●

## ファミコン

ファミコンは子どもたちを熱中させてしまうおもちゃ。学校から帰るとすぐゲームをはじめる

## マンガ

書店にはマンガのコーナーがあって、大量のマンガ本が売られている。マンガ本だけの専門店もある

売れるマンガ雑誌

電車の中でマンガを見るおとな。
日本独特の風景かも知れない

55

怪獣人気はおとろえない。おもちゃ売り場に並んださまざまな怪獣のモデル

# 遊園地

遊園地にはスピード、スリル、夢のある乗り物がいろいろある。子どもたちは、はじめての乗り物にこうふんし大喜び

# ●●● 現代文化 ●●●

## ● 日本の現代文学の作家たち

現代の日本の文学は、大きく３つにわけることができます。一番目は日本文学の独自性を出した谷崎潤一郎、川端康成、三島由紀夫といった作家たちです。川端康成が『雪国』でノーベル賞を受けたことは、よく知られています。

二番目は、世界文学の影響を受けて、自分たちの文学を普遍性のあるものとしてとらえ、世界に向けてフィードバックしようとしている大岡昇平、安倍公房、そして1994年にノーベル賞を受けた大江健三郎です。ノーベル賞の受賞理由で、川端の文学が「日本独特の情緒を描きだしている」と言われたのに対して、大江の文学が「世界的に普遍性のある問題を提起している」とされました。

三番目は吉本ばなな、村上春樹といった日本の現代の世相をサブカルチャーとしてとらえている文学です。最近は純文学の本が売れなくなったと言われます。これから日本文学はどのような方向に向かうのか、興味があります。

## ● 音楽

レコードからＣＤの時代に代わり、日本ではポピュラー音楽のＣＤがよく売れています。中には100万枚を超えるヒットもあります。どれも日本で作詞作曲された日本の歌手の歌です。

クラッシック音楽の分野では日本にも交響楽団がたくさんあり、あちこちで演奏会が開かれています。また海外からの音楽家の演奏会もよく行われています。しかし、音楽愛好家にとっては、演奏会の入場券が高いのが悩みの種です。場合によっては数万円のこともあります。これは国や地方公共団体の、文化面での助成が少ないことが原因の１つのようです。

また、優れた音楽家が多く生まれながら、かれらが主に海外で活躍しているのは残念なことです。東京のサントリーホールや大阪のフェスティバルホールといった音響効果のよい劇場では、常時演奏会が行われています。

## Contemporary Culture

### Modern Japanese Writing

Contemporary Japanese literature can be loosely divided into three categories. The first category is one in which the writings display the unique style of Japanese literature, represented by the works of writers such as Junichiro Tanizaki, Yasunari Kawabata and Yukio Mishima. Yasunari Kawabata, in particular, has gained much recognition for having been awarded the Nobel Prize for literature for his work which includes the well-known novel 'Snow Country'.

The second category describes a body of literature where writers, having been influenced by international literature and who look upon their own work as being universally valid, attempt to return a degree of 'feedback' to the outside world. Writers such as Shohei Ooka, Kobo Abe and Kenzaburo Oe (awarded the 1994 Nobel Prize for literature), fall into this grouping. Kawabata is said to have been awarded the Nobel prize for his 'portrayal of uniquely Japanese sentiments', while Oe's literature 'presents problems which reflect a global sense of universality'.

The third category of literature, represented by such writers as Banana Yoshimoto and Haruki Murakami, describes the social conditions of modern-day Japan as a kind of 'sub-culture'. Recently it has been reported that sales of serious literature have been declining. One cannot help but wonder about the direction of Japanese literature in the future.

### Music

Records have been replaced by CD's and the sales of popular music in Japan continue to do well. Some hit CD's have reportedly sold more than a million copies, the lyrics and music of such hits having been composed by Japanese singers in Japan.

When it comes to classical music, there is much activity in Japan. There are many symphony orchestras and concerts are a frequent occurrence. Furthermore, visiting international musicians often include Japan on their concert circuits. Unfortunately, however, exhorbitant admission prices to concerts are the cause of much anguish felt by music lovers. In some cases, a single ticket can cost tens of thousands of yen. A reason for such high prices might be the fact that subsidies for the arts provided by the national government or by local public organizations are few in number.

It is unfortunate that large numbers of distinguished Japanese musicians choose to work mainly overseas. Still, concert halls renowned for their fine acoustics, such as Tokyo's Suntory Hall and Osaka's Festival Hall continue to have busy concert programmes.

## ●美術

日本では最近、美術館がどんどん開館しています。1970年から1991年までに全国で県立、区立、町立や個人美術館など822あまりの美術館が開館しました。

またデパートにも美術館が併設されているところも多く、買い物帰りの人などでいつもいっぱいです。日本にいながら、世界の名画を見るチャンスがあるのは、とてもすばらしいことです。

日本人の住まいが洋風になったことで、絵を飾るスペースができ、居間に絵や版画を飾る家も増えています。自分の身近に絵を飾るという生活から、美術に対する関心が高まっているのかもしれません。

## ●映画

日本では、映画館で映画を見る人が減って、地方では閉館する映画館が増えています。都会の映画館も、平日のウイークデーは、人気の高い映画は別として、たいていはお客さんが少なくガラガラです。

それに対してレンタルビデオショップは、どんな地方の町に行っても必ず1軒か2軒はあります。好きな時間に好きな映画を楽しむという方が、現代人の生活のスタイルに合っているからでしょうか。

ビデオだけでなくテレビでも、毎日、さまざまな映画が放映されています。衛星放送では特に映画番組が多く「映画を見るために衛星放送をつける」という人もいるほどです。また映画番組専門のケーブルテレビもあります。

## ●企業メセナ

1990年にできた、財界人が文化や芸術を援助するシステムです。1口25万円で会員（準会員は12万円）になれます。約170の会社が会員で42社が準会員になっています。

日本の企業が、営利目的だけでなく、こういったボランティア事業にも参加するようになったというのは、1つの進歩に違いありません。

## Art

Recently in Japan, the number of art galleries being opened has been steadily growing. From 1970 to 1991, 882 art galleries (including prefectural, ward, town, and private) were opened throughout Japan.

In addition, numerous department stores have established galleries, as well. These are always crowded with people who drop in after they have finished their shopping. It is wonderful to be able to have this opportunity to see world masterpieces while still in Japan.

As Japanese houses have been becoming more Western in style, more space has become available to display works of art and as a result, more and more people are decorating their living rooms with paintings and prints. It may be said that, since people have become used to living with paintings around them, in their daily lives, there is a growing interest in art.

## Movies

In Japan, with the numbers of people going to see movies in movie theatres on the decrease, more and more local movie theatres are closing. Even in the cities, on week days movie theatres are usually almost empty, unless the movie playing proves to be especially popular.

Meanwhile, however, even if you go to a small country town, you will be sure to encounter one or two video rental shops. Perhaps the popularity of video may be put down to the fact that people in this day and age prefer the convenience of being able to watch whatever movie thay like, whenever they like.

One does not necessarily need to hire a video--various kinds of movies are screened every day on television. Satellite broadcasting channels show lots of movies, to the extent that there are people who subscribe to satellite broadcasting merely to be able to watch movies. There are also cable television stations which specialize in screening movies.

## Kigyo Mesena ('Corporate Subsidizing of the Art's)

This is a system which was established in 1990, whereby financiers contribute towards the support of cultural affairs and the arts. The price of a membership is 250,000 yen (associate memberships are 120,000 yen each). There are approximately 170 member companies and 42 associate member companies.

There is no doubt that the fact that Japanese corporations are becoming involved in such 'volunteer' schemes for non-profit motives is very much a positive step.

# ●●● 子ども文化 ●●●

現代社会の特徴の1つは出生数の減少です。1999年の調査では、日本の女性が生涯に生む子どもの数は、平均1.34人です。

子どもの数はますます少なくなり、ひとりっ子が増えています。兄弟げんかをしたこともなく、家に帰っても家族は両親だけ。しかも父親は会社人間で、家に帰ってきて寝るだけで、話し相手になってくれるのは母親だけという家庭が多いのです。そういう環境の中で子どもの文化が影響を受けていくのは当然といえます。

今、子どもの親になっている世代の多くは、日本が高度成長した後に育った人たちです。母親も子どもの育児のために、自分を犠牲にするのではなく、自分も楽しみたいという感覚を持っています。

家族でスキーを楽しみ、親と子でファミコンを楽しみ、マンガ雑誌を共有するという、以前には見られなかった親子関係が生まれてきつつあります。

## ● ファミコン

ファミコンはファミリーコンピュータの略です。はじめてファミコンが売り出されたのは1983年です。その時は宇宙から攻めてくる敵を打つシューティングゲームなどの、ごく単純なゲームが主でした。

ところが1987年ごろから、「ドラゴンクエスト」などのロールプレーゲームが出回り、デパートやおもちゃ屋では、それを買うために長い行列ができたほどです。

子どものゲームのために、父親が会社の帰りにおもちゃ屋に行ったり、母親がデパートの開店前から並んだりと、異常とも言える光景が新聞にも載りました。

1989年には携帯用ファミコンのゲームボーイが登場し、電車の中などでも子どもがファミコンで遊ぶ光景が、日常的に見られました。

1992年までにファミコンは1800万台、ゲームボーイ43万台、スーパーファミコン739万台も売られています 。これ

## The World of Children

One of the features of modern Japanese society is the declining birth rate. According to a 1999 survey, a Japanese woman will give birth to 1.34 children, on average, during her lifetime.

As the number of children declines, so the number of single child families increases. Only children will grow up never having experienced a quarrel with brothers or sisters. When they return home, the only family waiting to greet them will be their parents. What is more, since fathers devote so much of their time to the company and return home just to sleep, it is becoming increasingly common to find families where it is the mother who is the only person to talk to. It is only natural then, to assume that a child's interests will be influenced by this kind of environment.

Most parents today will have been brought up during the time when Japan was experiencing its rapid economic growth period. Rather than scacrificing themselves for the sake of the children, parents are beginning to sense that they want to derive some enjoyment from life.

Parents are developing new relationships with their children--skiing together as a family, playing computer games together and sharing comics--things unheard of in the past.

## Famikon (Computer Games)

Famikon is short for famirii kompyuuta ('family computer'), an electronic computer game. Famikon first went on sale in 1983. At that time, the games were mostly very straightforward 'shooting games involving invaders from outer space'.

However, in 1987, 'role-play' computer games , such as 'Dragon Quest', appeared on the market, causing long queues of purchasers to form at toy shops and department stores. There were newspaper accounts of extraordinary scenes of fathers calling in at toy shops on the way home from work and mothers lining up outside department stores before opening hours, all for the sake of acquiring such games.

In 1989 'Game Boy', a portable computer game, appeared and from this time children could be seen playing with computer games on trains and in other places.

To the year 1992, sales of 'Family Computer' were reported as 18,000,000 copies, 'Game Boy' 430,000 copies and 'Super Family Computer' as 7,390,000 copies. Such has been the infiltration of Famikon into the world of children, that those children without such computer games have diffi-

だけ子どもの世界にファミコンが浸透すると、ファミコンがないと仲間入りできないという現象もおき、そのことが「いじめ」の対象になったりさえしました。

これは日本だけの現象ではなく、海外にもそれぞれが数千万台ずつ出荷されています。

ファミコンは「子どものおもちゃ」から「子どもの必需品」へと変化していったようです。

おもちゃでは、テレビや雑誌に出てくるゴジラなど怪獣のプラモデルに、強い人気があります。

## ●マンガ文化

『少年マガジン』というマンガ雑誌があります。「少年」とつくからには、子ども用の雑誌に思えそうですが、実際には電車の中で高校生や大学生が読んでいたり、勤め帰りのサラリーマンが、駅の売店で買っている光景などが見られます。

販売数も420万冊といいますから、どんな本のベストセラーも追いつけないような数字です。しかもそのマンガが人から人の手にわたることを考えると、日本人の何人がこのマンガ雑誌を読んでいるのかと驚くほどです。

最近は、歴史や経済をマンガで教えたり、日本文学の古典である『源氏物語』や『枕草子』がマンガになったりしています。

また、消防庁や警視庁、自衛隊などの宣伝パンフレットにも、マンガを使ったものが出たりしています。こうなると、マンガは単なる娯楽ではなく、1つの情報伝達の方法になっています。それだけ活字離れがひどくなっているということでしょうか。

## ●遊園地

休みの日の遊園地は朝から子どもづれの家族でにぎわいます。新しい設備やスリルに富んだ乗り物の前では、順番を待つ人の長い行列ができます。乗り物のほかにもゲームや、レストランでの食事、買い物など、人びとは1日中楽しい時を過ごすことができます。

culty in making friends and in some cases, it has even been reported that this has become the object of bullying.

The popularity of computer games is not only a phenomenon peculiar to Japan-- each of the respective games has had foreign shipments amounting to tens of millions of copies. It appears' that Famikon has changed from being 'a child's toy' to being 'a child's essential'.

In the toy kingdom, plastic monster dolls and Godzilla models--'characters' from television and magazines, are enormously popular.

**The World of Comics**

There is a comic bearing the name Shonen Magajin ('Boys' Magazine). It might be considered that since the word 'boys' appears in the name of the comic, that it would be one for children. However, actually, it is not an unfamiliar sight to see highschool and university students reading it on trains, nor to see office workers buying it at station kiosks on the way home from work.

With sales of 4,200,000 copies, even a best-seller would have difficulty in competing with such figures. Furthermore, when you take into consideration the fact that people pass on comics to be read by others, the number of Japanese people reading this particular comic is truly staggering.

Using a comic format to teach history and economics is a further recent innovation. Classics of Japanese literature such as 'The Tale of Genji' and 'The Pillow Book of Sei Shonagon' have also been published in comic form.

In addition to this, the Fire Defence Agency, the Metropolitan Police Department and the Self-Defence Force use cartoons in their promotional pamphlets. In this way, cartoons may be perceived as not being merely a form of amusement but are being used as a means of disseminating information. Perhaps this is a further indication of how serious the problem of moving away from the written word is becoming.

**Amusement Parks**

On holidays, amusement parks present a lively scene from early in the morning, with family groups in large numbers. Long queues of people, waiting their turn, form in front of the latest attraction or thrilling ride. People are able to enjoy themselves all day--trying out the rides, playing games, eating in restaurants and shopping, among other things.

# 日本のスポーツ
## Japanese Sports

スポーツには見て楽しむスポーツと自分でするスポーツがあります。見るスポーツでは、野球・サッカー・相撲・ゴルフ・プロレス、自分が参加するスポーツでは、テニス・ゴルフ・野球・スキー・マリンスポーツが盛んです。

In the world of sports, there are spectator sports, and there are participatory sports. Sports that are enjoyable to watch include baseball, soccer, sumo, golf, and pro-wrestling, while tennis, golf, baseball, snow skiing, and marine sports are booming in recreational sports.

## サッカー

1993年、プロサッカーのJリーグが結成された。熱狂的なファンでうまったスタンド

"Jリーグ"商品も売り出され、人気をよんでいる

グランドではボールを追う少年たちの姿がめだつ

### 野球
プロサッカーができたが、プロ野球の人気も相変わらず続いている。
観客でいっぱいになった野球場

プロ選手のプレーは迫力がある。ホームインの瞬間

学校のグランドで、授業のあと、練習にはげむ高校の選手

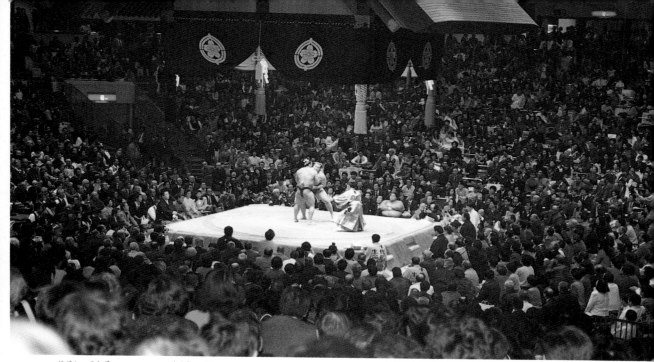

## 相撲
（すもう）

日本の国技といわれる相撲。丸い土俵の中で2人の力士が戦う。外国人のファンが増えている

## テニス

テニス人口は多い。若者、とくに女性にはファッショナブルなスポーツとして人気がある

## 柔道
（じゅうどう）

日本で始まった柔道も今や国際的、各国ですぐれた選手が出ている

# 空手
かって

空手は沖縄で、武器を持たない庶
民の武術として発達した。今は世
界に広まっている

手と足、頭など自分の体だけを使
った技で相手を倒す

# 剣道
けんどう

刀を使った剣術が、竹刀と防具をつけ
て試合をするように変わった。柔道と
共に授業に取り入れている学校もある

# 弓道
きゅうどう

弓に矢をつがえ、的をねらって放
つ弓道も日本に古くから伝わって
いる。的にあてる矢の本数で勝負

がきまる

# 日本のスポーツ

スポーツは自分自身で楽しむものであると同時に、ほかの人がするのを見て楽しむものでもあります。

スポーツの何が人気があるかを知るには、テレビ番組の中で占める時間の割合や、広場で遊ぶ子どもたちの遊び方、そして書店に並ぶ雑誌の特集などが、そのバロメーターになります。

1980年代までは、テレビで野球が占める時間は圧倒的に長く、また広場では子どもたちがよく野球をしていたものです。男の子のいる家庭には必ずといってよいくらい、バットやグローブがあったし、中学や高校の野球クラブの選手として活躍すれば、勉強はできなくてもヒーローでいることができました。

## ●サッカー

今、広場は少年サッカーの子どもたちでにぎわっています。また、スポーツニュースの時間にも、野球とサッカーは同じくらいの時間をとっています。これは1993年に設立されたプロサッカーリーグのJリーグが大人から子どもにまで大変な人気だからです。子どものお菓子や服にまで、「Jリーグ商品」がついていることからも、その人気がわかります。

Jリーグのシーズンは春から秋です。観客のことを考えて、試合は水曜日（春から夏にかけて）と土曜日を中心に行われます。現在（2000年）Jリーグは16チームあり、第1ステージと第2ステージに別れてリーグ戦をします。

日本ではそれほど人気のなかったサッカーがJリーグ設立いらい、爆発的な人気を得たのは、宣伝の力もずいぶん大きかったようです。

## ●野球

サッカーと人気を二分するようにはなりましたが、野球はまだまだ人気のあるスポーツです。特に夏の甲子園で行

---

Sport is something that the individual is able to enjoy by himself. At the same time, watching someone else play sport can also be enjoyable.

In order to find out just how popular sport really is, one only has to look at those things which act as a kind of 'barometer'--the proportion of time allotted to it in television programmes, children playing it outdoors and special features devoted to it in magazines for sale in bookstores.

Up until the 1980's, the amount of time taken up by baseball broadcasts on television was inordinately long. Similarly, children would often be seen playing baseball in open spaces. Wherever there were male children in the family, you would be guaranteed to find a baseball bat and catching glove, almost without fail. If boys joined the baseball clubs in junior or senior high schools, even if they weren't particularly good scholars, they could attain 'hero' status.

### Soccer

These days playing areas are crowded with young boys playing soccer. Sports news programmes allocate equal lengths of time to baseball and soccer. The establishment of a professional soccer league--the 'J League', in 1993, which has proved to be hugely popular with young and old alike, is the reason for this change. The fact that there are even children's sweets and clothing bearing the 'J League' logo testifies to the popularity of the sport.

The J League season runs from spring through to autumn. Taking into consideration the convenience of spectators, matches take place, in the main, on Wednesdays (from spring through the summer) and on Saturdays. Presently there are sixteen teams that participate in the league series, the season being divided into two stages--'First' and 'Second Stage'.

In the past, soccer as a sport has never been particularly popular. The tremendous popularity that soccer has gained since the establishment of the J League seems to be attributable to the large amount of promotion that has been undertaken.

### Baseball

While baseball has had to share half of the popularity stakes with soccer, it is still very much a popular sport in Japan. In particular, the Senior High School Baseball Series which takes place in Koshien is said to be a national event. The players at this event are from high schools which have been selected to represent urban and rural prefectures and so, with the sense of baseball and love for one's home province being united, squads of fans flock to Koshien from country areas.

われる高校野球は、国民的な行事と言えます。都道府県の代表の高校から選手が出るため、郷土愛と野球が一体となり、甲子園には地方から応援団が駆けつけます。

日本のプロ野球は12球団あります。1950年に創立されたセントラル・リーグ（セリーグ）とパシフィック・リーグ（パリーグ）です。セリーグとパリーグでそれぞれペナントを競って130試合戦い、リーグで優勝したチームが日本シリーズで戦います。最近では各球団に外国人選手がいて、日本人選手と協力しながら活躍しています。

## ●相撲

日本の相撲は『古事記』や『日本書紀』の神話時代にも出てくるほど、昔からあるスポーツです。その後、奈良時代になると、朝廷の行事として相撲を見ることにしました。今でも『天覧相撲』といって、国技館に天皇・皇后両陛下が観覧にいらっしゃいます。そして鎌倉時代、武士の社会になると武士たちが相撲を奨励しました。そして相撲はだんだんプロフェッショナルな仕事へとなっていき、江戸時代には職業力士が登場します。

日本の国技である相撲は、本場所が１年に６場所もあります。初場所（１月）、夏場所（５月）、秋場所（９月）は東京の国技館で、春場所（３月）は大阪、そして名古屋場所（７月）と九州場所（11月）があります。力士たちは試合に全力をそそぎ、その合間は稽古と毎日大変な生活です。

力士になるためには義務教育を終えた人で、身長が173センチ、体重が75キロ以上なければなれません。しかしこの基準は、最近体格のよくなった日本人には、それほどきびしいものではありません。

力士はまげを結い、土俵にあがる時には腰のまわりにまわしをしめます。

力士の資格に「日本人であること」という規定はなく、1993年には曙が外国人としてはじめて横綱になりました。曙は髷がとてもよく似合います。これからも、外国人力士が日本の相撲に増えていくかもしれませんね。

力士は上位から横綱、大関、関脇、小結、前頭と強さに

In the Japanese professional baseball league there are twelve corporations which own a professional baseball team. The system which was founded in 1950, consists of the 'Central League' (Se Riigu), and the 'Pacific League' (Pa Riigu). The teams of each league compete for the pennant through a series of 130 matches. Then the two league championship teams play off in the 'Japan Series'. These days, there are foreign players in each of the professional baseball teams who, playing side by side their Japanese team mates, take a keen part in the action.

**Sumo Wrestling**

Japanese sumo wrestling is a sport dating from ancient times and is even referred to in the **Kojiki** ('Legendary Stories of Old Japan') and the **Nihon Shoki** ('Chronicles of Japan') from the mythical age of Japanese history. Later, during the Nara Period, the viewing of sumo wrestling became an Imperial Court rite. Even today, both the Emperor and Empress visit the **Kokugikan** ('National Sport Arena') to view sumo. These occasions are known as **tenran zumo** ('Command Wrestling Matches for the Emperor'). In the Kamakura Period, when the society was one of **samurai** warriors, the **samurai** encouraged sumo wrestling. Sumo then gradually began to take on the attributes of a profession and in the Edo Period, the first professional sumo wrestlers appeared.

Sumo wrestling, the national sport of Japan, has six regular tournaments a year. These are: the New Year's Grand Sumo Tournament in January, the summer tourney in May and the autumn tournament in September, all of which are held at the Kogugikan in Tokyo. Then there are the spring sumo tournament in March, held in Osaka and the Nagoya and Kyushu Tournaments which take place in July and November, respectively. The wrestlers bring all their strength into play in their tournament matches. In between tournaments the regimen of daily training makes for a gruelling existence.

In order to become a sumo wrestler one must have completed compulsory education, be at least 173 centimetres tall and weigh in excess of 75 kilograms. With younger Japanese having better physiques these days, meeting these standards is not as hard as it used to be.

Sumo wrestlers wear their hair in a topknot and when they appear in the ring they wear a special loincloth or belt known as a **mawashi**.

There is no stipulation that, in order to become a sumo wrestler, you must be Japanese and in 1993, a foreign wrestler called Akebono ('New Dawn') became the first non-Japanese to reach the rank of grand champion. Akebono strikes quite a pose with his hair in a topknot. The numbers of foreign wrestlers joining the sumo ranks in Japan will probably continue to grow in the years ahead.

The ranks of wrestlers are strictly divided according to wrestling ability.

よってその地位が細かく別れています。

　勝負は、どちらかの力士の体の一部分が土に触れたり土俵から押し出されたりした方が負けです。1場所は15日間で、力士は毎日違う相手と対戦します。

　横綱や大関は、ある程度地位が保証されています。しかし、それ以下の力士は1場所ごとの成績によって、地位が上がったり下がったりします。勝負の世界はきびしいものです。

## ●テニス

　テニスは年代をこえて人気のあるスポーツです。高校や大学のクラブでもテニス部員は多く、休日のテニスコートはどこもプレーをする人でいっぱいです。選手権試合のような大きなゲームは、よくテレビでも放送されます。

## ●柔道

　日本で始まったスポーツが世界的なものになった代表格が柔道です。現在世界で柔道の愛好者は600万人と言われています。私がイギリスにいた時には、大学のクラブでも柔道がさかんで柔道着を着た若者たちが、日本語で「礼」「はじめ」などと言っているのを見てうれしく思ったものです。1951年に結成された「国際柔道連盟」International Judo Federation に1994年には152か国が参加しています。

　東京にある講道館は、柔道の祖、嘉納治五郎が1882年に講道館柔道を始めた場所です。当時は畳12畳に門人がたった9人でした。でも現在の道場は大道場が420畳もあり、学校道場が240畳など、全部で1272畳もあります。入門者の数は全国で160万人以上ということですから、いかに柔道の人気が高いかがわかります。柔道の試合はずっと長い間体重に関係なく行われてきました。しかし1964年に東京オリンピックの正式種目になる時、ヨーロッパ諸国の強い主張で体重別に変わりました。

　柔道は男性ばかりのものではありません。女子柔道の試合は1974年にオセアニア女子選手権大会が初めてで、その後世界の各地で開かれています。

These are in order: Yokozuna ('Grand Champion'), Ozeki ('Champion'), Sekiwake ('Champion 2nd Class'), Komusubi ('Champion 3rd Class') and Maegashira ('Senior Wrestler').

In a sumo match, the wrestler who has any part of his body touch the ring surface, or, who is pushed out of the ring, is the loser. One tournament lasts for fifteen days with wrestlers pitting their strength against a different opponent every day.

There is a certain inherent status guaranteed with the ranks of yokozuna and ozeki. However, for wrestlers below these ranks, one's performance in each tournament will determine whether one is promoted or demoted. The competitive world of sumo is certainly a tough one!

## Tennis

Tennis is a sport popular with all generations. Tennis clubs in high schools and universities enjoy large memberships, and public courts on weekends are full of people absorbed in play. Large tennis tournaments such as Championship matches are frequently televised in Japan.

## Judo

Judo, a sport which began in Japan, has attained world-class recognition. At present there are reported to be six million devotees of the sport throughout the world. When I was in England, the judo club at my university was popular, too, and I remember watching with delight the young people in their judo suits, as they shouted in Japanese Rei ('Bow!') and Hajime ('Begin!').

In 1951 the International Judo Federation was formed and today has a membership of 152 participating nations.

The Kodokan in Tokyo is the place where the founder of judo, Jigoro Kano first established the Kodokan School of judo, in 1882. At that time the hall was a twelve tatami mat affair and there were only nine students. Today, however, there is a large judo hall of 420 mats and a judo hall for teaching purposes with 240 mats. In all, there is an area the equivalent of 1272 mats. That judo continues to enjoy wide popularity is revealed in the fact that there are more than one and a half million pupils of judo nationwide.

For many years judo matches took place without any consideration being given to the weights of the exponents. But in 1964, when judo became an official event at the Tokyo Olympics, weight classes were instituted at the insistence of European nations.

Judo is not a male-dominated sport. The first women's judo matches took place at the Oceania Women's Championships in 1974 and since this time, Women's Judo has been practised throughout the world.

Judo is said to be a 'contest of techniques (waza)'. These techniques are broadly divided into three kinds--nagewaza, throwing techniques, katamewaza, holds which render the opponent immobile on the floor and atemiwaza, knockdown blows.

柔道は「技の勝負」と言われます。技は大きく分けると「投げ技」「固め技」「当て身技」の３つです。その中で当て身技は、相手の急所をこぶしなどで狙うもので、危険ということで試合では禁止されています。技は細かく分けると全部で80以上もあります。

柔道は柔道着を着て行われます。また初心者は白帯、１、２、３級は茶色帯、初段から５段は黒帯、６段から８段は赤白帯、一番強い９段、10段が赤帯と、帯の色で区別するようになっています。

## ●空手

中国から沖縄へ伝わり、武器を持たない護身術として発達したものです。拳や手、足を使って、相手を突き、打ち、蹴るなどの技があります。

## ●剣道

剣道は竹刀を使って２人で行うものです。剣道は「礼にはじまり礼に終わる」と言われます。試合を見ていると、両膝を折って、竹刀を中断にかまえるところから始まります。これは相手の人格を尊重することを表す大切な作法で、厳粛な雰囲気が漂います。

剣道の試合は３本勝負が原則で、試合時間内に２本先取した方が勝ちになります。代表的な構えは５つあり、上段、中段、下段、八相、脇で、これを「五行の構え」と言います。

剣道では、相手をまるで遠くの山を見るように、相手の全体をとらえ、外見だけではなく内面をとらえるのが大切ということです。

## ●弓道

弓道も日本古来の伝統ある武道の一つです。両足先を開いて立ち、的に向かって矢をしぼり、的に向かって一直線に矢を放ちます。近的（28㍍）と遠的（60㍍）競技があります。日本の弓道人口は約100万人です。

Of these, the use of **atemiwaza** in matches is not allowed, since it entails striking with the fist at the opponent's vital points, which is considered dangerous. In all, when all the 'techniques' are categorized, they number more than eighty.

Judo is performed while wearing a judo suit, known as a judogi. The colour of the belt worn with the suit indicates the rank-- beginners wear a white belt, the first three **kyu** ('classes') wear a brown belt, the first to the fifth **dan** ('grade') wear a scarlet and white belt and the highest levels, those of the 9th and 10th dan, wear a scarlet belt.

### Karate

Karate, literally meaning 'empty- handed', was originally a form of unarmed self-defense which came from China by way of Okinawa. It involves techniques of thrusting (tsuki), striking (uchi) and kick- ing (keri) when confronting the opponent, using the fists, hands and legs.

### Kendo ('Japanese Fencing')

Kendo is practised by two players using bamboo swords. It is said that a kendo match always begins and ends with the word rei ('Bow!'). When one is watching a match the action begins with both players in a squatting position, their shinai ('bam- boo swords') at middle guard. This impor- tant etiquette is meant to suggest the act of attuning oneself to the opponent's char- acter and at this time a feeling of solem- nity hangs in the air.

Kendo matches operate upon the princi- ple of 'best of three' and if a player achieves the advantage of two consecutive wins within the allotted time, he is the outright winner. There are five representa- tive postures in kendo, known as Gogyoo no kamae, namely jodan ('holding a sword over one's head'), chudan ('with one's sword at middle guard'), gedan ('holding one's sword low'), hasso ('sword held on the right side of the body, pointing up') and waki de ('with one's sword held on the right hand side of the body pointing down').

In kendo one looks at one's opponent as if he were a far-away mountain. Taking in one's opponent as a whole--not merely the outward appearance, but capturing the inner essence, is said to be important.

### Kyudo ('Japanese Archery')

Kyudo is also an art which originates from a traditional ancient Japanese mar- tial art form. A person stands with feet apart, draws an arrow back and, facing the target, shoots the arrow directly at it. There are two competitive events--the short course (28 metres) and the long course (60 metres). There are approximate- ly one million people in Japan who prac- tise Kyudo.

# 日本の教育
## Japanese Education

日本は、小学校と中学校が義務教育ですが、その上の高等学校への進学率は95％に達する高学歴社会です。また、就職を有利にするには、有名大学に進学しなければならないということで、その準備で小学生の頃から受験競争が始まります。

Japan is an "education society" where 95% of all students advance into high school, even though only elementary and middle school are compulsory. Also, because graduation from a famous university is necessary in order to find a good job, preparation begins around elementary school for grueling entrance examinations.

小学校の授業風景。子どもの数が少なくなり、1クラスの人数も40人を切るようになった

男女の小学生。私立校の多くは制服がある。私立の有名高校や大学に付属している学校は入学希望者が多く競争率が高い

69

大人の仲間入りをした
大学生たちは、自由な
生活を楽しんでいる

大学のキャンパスも女子学生が増
えた。文学部のように女性のほう
が多い学部もある

学生たちは、おもいお
もいに席をとって講義
を聞いている

※医学部・歯学部は
大学6年、大学院4年

**日本の学校制度**

| | | | 博士課程 3年 |
|---|---|---|---|
| | 大学院 | | 修士課程 2年 |

| 専門学校 1～3年 | | 4年 | 大学 | | 短期大学 2年 | | 高等 1～5年 |
|---|---|---|---|---|---|---|---|
| 高等学校 3年 | | | | | | 高等 専修学校 | |
| 中学校 3年 | | | | | | | |
| 小学校 6年 | | | | | | | |
| 幼稚園 | | | | | | | |

# 日本の宗教
にほん　しゅうきょう

## Religion in Japan

日本の宗教は仏教と神道が二大宗教といえます。しかしお正月に神社に行き、お盆にはお寺に行く、また同じ家の中に神棚と仏壇があって、その両方に手を合わせて拝むというように、二つの宗教は日本人の信仰のなかにとけ合っているといえます。

It is said that Buddhism and Shinto are Japan's two religions. However, because the Japanese worship at Shinto shrine's at New Year's, and at Buddhist temples at obon, and Japanese homes often have a small household Shinto shrine, as well as a much larger Buddhist altar, it can be said that these two faiths have come together in the beliefs of the Japanese.

お寺参りにきた人びと。正面の本堂の両側にお守りやおみくじの売り場がならんでいる（右）

地蔵尊はお地蔵さまといって古くから庶民の身近な信仰の対照（下）

有名なお寺や神社のまわりには食べ物やおみやげを売る店が出ている（下右）

71

神社には神が祭ってある。神社の入り口には門として鳥居が立つ

拝殿で鈴をならし、おさいせんをあげて祈る

▲神社やお寺では、拝む前に、手を洗って清めるならわしがある

▼神前で行う神前結婚式。神社だけでなく、ホテルや結婚式場でも行える

# 日本の教育

## ●高学歴社会

日本の教育は小学校6年、中学校3年、高等学校3年、大学4年の6・3・3・4制と呼ばれる制度をとっています。中学校までが義務教育ですが、高等学校進学率は、96パーセントにも達し、高等学校卒業は当然という感じです。大学進学率は43パーセントで、日本は世界でも有数の高学歴社会となっています。

一流大学をめざすために一流高校へ、そのためには一流中学や一流小学校へと受験競争は過熱する一方で、幼稚園から予備校に通う子どももいるほどです。

有名小学校を受験したいのは子ども本人ではありません。子どもは受験勉強するよりも、遊んでいたいものだと思います。ところが子どもの両親にとっては、子どもを良い小学校へ入れることは、将来、有名大学に進む道が約束されたように思えるのでしょう。なぜなら、有名小学校の大部分が有名大学につながる私立だからです。両親までが小学校受験の時の「両親の面接」の準備をするといった、笑えない現象まで起きています。

これらは、日本が学歴社会であるために起きた現象で、誰もがおかしいと思いながら、この受験競争に巻き込まれているのが現状です。

## ●子どもの巣ごもり

学校が終わると、そのまま塾に直行し、そして家では自分の部屋でテレビを見たり、ファミコンをしたりする子どもが増えています。「子どもたちの巣ごもり」と呼ばれる現象です。アメリカの心理学者ハビー・ガーストによれば、子どもたちにはその年齢にふさわしい行動がある(developmental task)とされています。たとえば小学生なら、友達と仲良くする、男女によって行動が違うことを覚える、など9つがあげられています。

昔は年齢の違う子どもたちが空き地でいっしょに遊んだ

## Japanese Education

### A Well-Educated Society

Education in Japan is based upon what is referred to as the 6. 3. 3. 4 system-- namely six year of primary education, three years of junior high school and three years of senior high school, followed by four years of university. Children receive compulsory education until the end of junior high school. The percentage of students continuing on to senior high school is as much as 96 per cent. In fact, there is a feeling that having graduated from senior high school is a foregone conclusion. With 43 per cent of high school graduates going on to university, Japan occupies a very high place in the world as a well-educated society.

To aim for a top-ranking university one must aim for a top-ranking senior high school. To enter one of these, one aims for a first-class junior high school and primary school, in turn--the competition on entrance examinations for such schools is becoming increasingly fierce, to such an extent that there are even children of kindergarten age attending preparatory schools.

It is not just the children themselves who are keen to take entrance examinations for well-known primary schools. Rather than studying for entrance examinations, children would prefer to be enjoying themselves. However, the parents of the children perhaps feel that having the children enter good primary schools is a sure guarantee of a future place in a well-known university. The reason for this is that a majority of well-known primary schools are private schools connected to distinguished universities. The situation is so serious, in fact, that there are even parents who prepare themselves for 'parental interviews' which take place at the time of primary school entrance examinations.

These circumstances are a direct result of Japan being a society which places great importance upon academic background--as absurd as anyone may think, the situation being inextricably tied up with the competitive world of entrance examinations is the existing state of affairs.

### The 'Nesting' of Children

The number of children who, school over, make their way directly to tutoring school, then, once they reach home, retreat to their rooms to watch television and play video games, is on the increase. This phenomenon is referred to as the 'nesting' of Japanese children.

The American psychologist Harvey Garst talks of children having 'developmental tasks'--behaviour to be learned appropriate to their age. For example, to cite but two of the nine 'tasks' put forward:

ものです。その中で必ずリーダーになる子どもがいて、子どもたちは子どもの社会を作り上げていました。ところが今はこういった「遊びの集団のリーダー」の姿を見つけるのはむずかしいのです。

## ●教科書検定制度

小学校、中学校、高等学校の教科書は文部省の検定教科書が使われ、指導内容がまえもって文部省からチェックされます。それは原稿本審査、修正合格、合格という段階を踏みます。日本の歴史の教科書の書き方をめぐって、「教科書裁判」などが起き、検定制度が一部改定されましたが、まだ文部省の強い検定権は残っています。

## ●校則のきびしさ

中学校や高校で最近問題になっているのは「校則がきびしいこと」でしょう。生徒の行動を１つの型にはめようとする校則は、自分で判断し解決しようとする力を奪い、自主性のない生徒を育てます。日本の社会が集団志向と言われる原因の１つが、この教育のシステムにあるようです。学校教育の中でよく言われる「みんなと同じ行動をしなさい」「１人だけ特別なことをしてはいけません」といった教師の言葉が、伸びようとする個性を殺してしまう結果になるのです。

## ●日本の大学生

大学生は、日本の社会の中で一番恵まれた存在かもしれません。高校までの先生の管理の目から離れ、親からは大人として扱われます。今まで出来なかった、アルバイトをする、遊びたいだけ遊ぶ、寝たいだけ寝る、興味のない授業には出ないということも、することができます。こういった自由の中で、クラブでスポーツに夢中になる、アルバイトでお金をためて車を買ったり海外旅行するなど、変化に富んだ生活を楽しんでいます。「大学のレジャーランド化」と言われるのも当然かもしれません。そんな中でも、もちろん専門の研究を熱心に勉強する大学生もいます。

children of primary school age learning how to get on with friends, and learning about the different behavioural patterns of boys and girls.

Children of various age-groups used to play together in open spaces. There would always be one child who was the leader and the children would create their own kind of society. However, these days, it is difficult to find the leader in a group of playing children.

**The Authorized Textbook System**

Primary schools, and junior and senior high schools in Japan use textbooks which are authorized by the Ministry of Education. The teaching content of such textbooks is closely scrutinized by the Ministry. This Ministry inspection involves a number of stages--manuscript inspection, acceptance with revisions and finally, acceptance. A 'School Textbook Hearing' was held concerning the writing of textbooks for Japanese history, with the result that the authorization system was partially revised. Nevertheless, the presence of Ministerial authorization is still strongly felt.

**Strict School Rules**

A recent problem that has come to light in Senior High Schools is that of the 'strictness of school rules'. School rules that attempt to regiment the behaviour of senior high school students into a single pattern deprive such students of the ability to judge and solve for themselves, fostering individuals who lack a sense of independence. It would seem to be an undeniable fact that the very nature of the education system contributes to the reason for Japanese society being described as 'group-oriented'.

Statements frequently used by teachers in school education such as 'Act like everyone else!' and 'Don't do anything that draws attention to yourself!' have a negative effect on the development of the individual.

**University Students in Japan**

University students could be said to have the most privileged existence in Japanese society. No longer under the watchful eye of school teachers, they are treated by their parents as adults. Now, at last, they are able to do the things they have previously been unable to--hold part-time jobs, enjoy themselves as much as they like, sleep as long as they wish and not attend classes that don't interest them. Faced with such freedom, college students enjoy a life-style full of changes, whether it be becoming involved in a university sports club, or, saving up earnings from a part-time job to buy a car, or go on an overseas trip. It might seem only natural to 'think of Japanese universities as leisure centres'. Needless to say, there are, of course, university students who are keenly involved in specialized areas of study.

# 日本の宗教

日本の宗教は、日本に古くからある神道と外国から入ってきた仏教が、生活の基本にあります。この２つの宗教はお互いにまじりあって、独特の神仏信仰を生み出してきました。日本人の家庭には神棚と仏壇がある家がよくあります。外国人は、神棚に向かって拝み、祖先をまつった仏壇に向かって拝む日本人を不思議に思うようです。

キリスト教は、江戸時代の徹底的な迫害の歴史を経て、近代以降は主に、知識人階層に受け入れられてきました。しかし、その数は人口のわずか１パーセントの110万人にすぎません。

たとえどの宗教を信じようと、民衆のレベルの宗教意識は、悪いことはしない、良いことをすれば天国（極楽）に行けるといった普遍的なパターンを持っているようです。

初もうでは神社に行き、結婚式は教会であげ、お葬式はお寺で行う、こういったことを矛盾と感じないのが、日本人の宗教観といえます。

## ●仏教

仏教は紀元前５世紀ごろインドで始まり、６世紀に中国から朝鮮半島を通って日本に来たものです。聖徳太子が仏教を保護し、その後たくさんのお寺が日本中に建てられました。そして鎌倉時代になると、一部のエリートのための宗教から、民衆の宗教へとなっていきました。法然、親鸞、道元、日蓮といったお坊さんが、民衆にもわかりやすい道を説いたからです。徳川時代は幕府の保護を受けて大きく発展しましたが、現在では、先祖の供養を主にする「葬式仏教」の面を強くしています。

現在、日本には約７万５千のお寺があり、お坊さんの数は18万人、信徒は８千万人ほどです。

## ●神道

神道は、自然に対して崇拝する気持ちが宗教となったも

# Religion in Japan

Japanese religions, namely Shintoism, an ancient Japanese system of beliefs and Buddhism, a religion which came from foreign parts, are fundamental to everyday life. These two religions have co-mingled and produced a distinctive system of Shintoist and Buddhist beliefs.

In Japanese houses it is common to find kamidana, a household Shinto altar and Butsudan, a family Buddhist altar. Foreigners seem to find it strange that Japanese pray before the household Shinto altar and do the same before the Buddhist altar which enshrines family ancestors. Christianity, having undergone the utter persecution of the Edo Period, has predominantly gained the acceptance of the intelligentsia, in modern times. However, the number of Christians amounts to only 1 per cent of Japan's population-- approximately 1.1 million people.

No matter what religion one believes in, the religious consciousness of the general public seems to possess a universal pattern--the practise of not doing wrong and the fact that good behaviour enables one to go to 'Heaven' or 'Paradise' (in the case of Buddhism).

Visiting a Shinto shrine at New Year, having a wedding ceremony in a Christian church and having a funeral service conducted in a Buddhist temple--these things do not strike Japanese people as being contradictory, but in fact, may serve to give a clearer picture of their 'religious outlook'.

## Buddhism

Buddhism originated in India in the 5th Century BC and later, in the 6th Century, came to Japan from China by way of the Korean Peninsula. Shotoku Taishi became a patron of Buddhism and from this time many temples were erected throughout Japan. By the time of the Kamakura Period, from being a religion practised by a few elite members, Buddhism had become the religion of the masses. The teaching of the priests Honen, Shinran, Dogen and Nichiren, easily understood by the public at large, made this possible. During the Tokugawa Period, Buddhism flourished, enjoying the patronge of the shogunate, however, these days, emphasis is placed on 'Funeral Buddhism' which chiefly involves memorial services for ancestors.

Presently in Japan there are about 75,000 Buddhist temples, 180,000 Buddhist priests and as many as 80 million followers of Buddhism.

## Shintoism

Shintoism is a religion which developed from a kind of nature worship and may be described as a form of animism. The reli-

ので、アニミズム（animism）の一種と言えるでしょう。アニミズムは動物、植物、自然現象の中に精霊があるという、宗教的な考え方です。

　神道は、初期のころには開祖も教理もありませんでしたが、仏教や儒教とまじりあううちに社殿を造ったり教理を教えるようになっていったのです。今、神社は日本全国に８万あり、信徒の数は１億人とされていますが、実際のところはわかりません。初もうでや結婚式などの時には神社に行く人が多いのです。また近代的なホテルの中にも結婚式のために小さな神社が造られ、そこで神主さんが祝詞をあげてくれます。

　神社は鳥居がその目印です。都会では神社が姿を消してしまったように思えますが、ビルの屋上などの思わぬところに鳥居がたっていることもあります。

## ● 地蔵信仰

　もともとはインドの神様でしたが、日本では平安時代から修行するお坊さんの姿をして、民衆を救うとされていました。また中世以降は、民間の信仰とまじりあい、村境や辻にたてられています。

　「村のはずれのお地蔵さんは、いつもニコニコ見てござる」（童謡より）

　赤いよだれかけをしたお地蔵さんは、どこかユーモラスで子どもたちに親しまれるのでしょう。童謡や童話の中にもよく登場します。お地蔵さんは子どもが大好きということで「子育て地蔵」も各地にたくさんあります。

## ● 修験道

　原始的な山岳信仰と密教がいっしょになったものです。人の住まない山の奥で、超人的な修行を積んで霊力を身につけた人を山伏といいます。今でも紀伊半島の熊野や東北の出羽三山は、山伏が修行する場所として有名です。出羽三山では３日間コースや１週間の修行コースがあります。現在のぜいたくな生活を反省するためにも、山で修行してみるのもよいかもしれません。

gious view of animism is that every animal, plant and natural phenomenon possesses a spirit.

In the early stages of Shintoism there was no founder, nor was they any doctrine, but as it mixed with Buddhism and ascetic practises, sanctuaries were built and the teaching of doctrine developed. Today, there are 80,000 Shinto shrines throughout Japan, and the number of Shinto followers is reported to be 100 million, however it is difficult to verify this. The fact remains that many people visit Shinto shrines for their first pilgrimage of the year and for wedding ceremonies. In addition to this, small shrines for wedding services are to be found in modern hotels, where Shinto priests recite prayers for the newlyweds.

The torii ('Shinto shrine gate') indicates the presence of a Shinto shrine. In cities, one may think that shrines have disappeared without a trace, however it is possible to encounter torii in unexpected places--on the roofs of buildings, for instance.

### Belief in Jizo ('Guardian Deities of Children)

Originally, Jizo was an Indian god. In Japan, during the Heian Period he assumed the guise of a Buddhist priest doing ascetic training and was believed to be the deliverer of the people. Later in the Middle Ages, the practises of Jizo worship mixed with folk beliefs and Jizo statues came to be erected at village boundaries and crossroads.

Threre is a children's song that goes: 'On the outskirts of the village the jizo-san is always keeping an eye on us, with a smile on his face.'

Guardian deities, with their red bibs, have a somewhat humorous appearance, which earns them the affection of children. Jizo often appear in children's songs and nursery tales. Since jizo-san is reputed to have a great affection for children, kosodate jizo or 'child-raising Jizo' statues are found throughout the country.

### Shugendo ('Mountain Ascetism')

Shugendo derives from a combination of a primitive faith which embraces mountains and esoteric Buddhism. A person who has acquired spiritual strength which is the result of superhuman ascetic training undergone deep in the remotest part of the mountains, is known as a yamabushi ('mountain priest'). Even today, Kumano in the Kii Peninsula and Dewa Sanzan in the Tohoku region are renowned as places where yamabushi undergo ascetic training. Priests at Dewa Sanzan run three-day and one-week yamabushi training courses. Undertaking an ascetic training course in the mountains might be an effective way of allowing us to reflect upon our present extravagant lifestyles.

# 日本の政治
## Japanese Government

日本の政治は三権分立制です。立法権は国会、行政権は内閣、司法権は裁判所が、それぞれ受けもっています。内閣の長である内閣総理大臣は国会が指名、最高裁判所長官は内閣が指名、国会議員は選挙で、国民である有権者の直接投票によって選ばれるしくみです。

The political power in Japan is divided among three branches of government. The legislative power resides in the Diet, the executive power in the Cabinet, and the judicial power in the courts. The Diet selects the Prime Minister, who is the head of the Cabinet. The Cabinet selects the Chief Justice of the Supreme Court, and citizens eligible to vote choose Diet members in an election.

国会の議事が行われる「国会議事堂」とその内部。中央奥の高い所が議長、その左側に並ぶのが内閣総理大臣以下各省の大臣。丸く取りかこむように国会議員席がある

選挙になると、立候補者の選挙運動が始まる。有権者と握手しながら支援を求める

運動員をしたがえ、宣伝カーの上から演説、有権者に訴える

立候補すると、区域内の指定個所にポスターをはり、選挙運動が始まる

国会

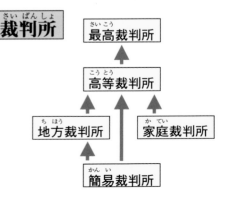

| 衆議院 | 参議院 |
|---|---|
| 定数 480人 | 定数 252人 |
| 任期 4年 | 任期 6年 |
| (解散がある) | (3年ごとに半数を改選) |

裁判所

最高裁判所

↑

高等裁判所

↑

地方裁判所　家庭裁判所

↑

簡易裁判所

行政

内閣

内閣総理大臣
各国務大臣

| 環境省 | 国土交通省 | 経済産業省 | 農林水産省 | 厚生労働省 | 文部科学省 | 財務省 | 外務省 | 法務省 | 総務省 | 金融庁 | 防衛庁 | 国家公安委員会 | 内閣府 |
|---|---|---|---|---|---|---|---|---|---|---|---|---|---|

# 日本の経済
## The Japanese Economy

日本は高度経済成長によって経済大国になりましたが、1991年をピークに成長はとまり、景気は後退しました。貿易黒字からくる外国との経済摩擦、円高、産業構造の変化などの難問をかかえ、これをどう解決していくかが、日本経済の課題になっています。

Japan became an economic superpower through a period of rapid economic growth. In 1991, however, the expansion reached a peak, and the business climate turned down. The topic of how to resolve the difficult problems of the economic friction with other countries resulting from trade surpluses, of the strong yen, of the changing industrial framework, and so on, has become a central issue in Japan's economy.

東京証券取引所。(月曜から金曜までの午後1時30分から英語による外国人見学ツアーを行っている)

日本の工業製品を代表する自動車
は輸出額も大きい。港で船積みを
待つ車

オートメーション化により
車の大量生産がすすんだ

海外旅行をする人が増え、空港の
ロビーはいつも混雑している

新しく建つビルは、時代に合わせ
てインテリジェントビルが多い

## 日本の貿易

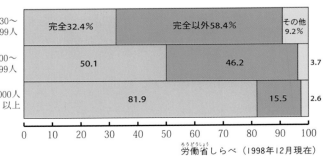

「通商白書」より

## 企業規模別の週休2日制の状況

| | | | |
|---|---|---|---|
| 30〜99人 | 完全32.4% | 完全以外58.4% | その他9.2% |
| 100〜999人 | 50.1 | 46.2 | 3.7 |
| 1000人以上 | 81.9 | 15.5 | 2.6 |

労働省しらべ（1998年12月現在）

80

# 日本の政治

<ruby>日本<rt>に ほん</rt></ruby>の<ruby>政治<rt>せい じ</rt></ruby>

## ●日本国憲法

日本国憲法は、1946年にそれまであった大日本帝国憲法を改正する形で公布され、1947年から施行されています。この憲法は、戦後、日本がアメリカに占領されている時にできたものです。

現在の日本国憲法は、前文と天皇、戦争の放棄、国民の権利と義務、国会、内閣、司法、などについて103か条が決められています。それまでの明治憲法と違う点は、天皇ではなく国民に主権があること、平和主義を強調したこと、国民の基本的人権を保障したことなどです。

基本的人権には、はじめ信教の自由、思想・良心の自由、出版・言論の自由などと共に、国民の1人1人が人間らしい生活をすることを国家に要求する権利（生存権）や、プライバシーの権利なども含まれています。コンピュータの発達と共に、プライバシーの保護制度が必要になり、1988年「個人情報保護法」が公布されています。

## ●国会

国会は日本のただ一つの立法機関で、衆議院と参議院よりなります。衆議院の議員数は480人、参議院の議員数は252人です。この中で婦人議員の割合は2000年には10.7%で世界で少ない方です。日本の政治が男性によって行われていることがよくわかります。

1993年の細川内閣で、衆議院議員の議長に女性の土井たか子氏が選ばれ、大臣にも女性が登場し、日本の政治にも女性参加が強く印象づけられました。これから、国会にも女性議員が多く登場することになると思います。

## ●選挙

議員は国民の選挙によって選ばれます。選挙の時になると各市町村から、20歳以上の有権者に投票用紙が配達され、25歳以上になると被選挙権を持つようになります。

---

## Japanese Government

### The Constitution of Japan

The present Constitution of Japan is an amended form of the 'Constitution of the Empire of Japan' which was in force prior to 1946. The present constitution was promulgated post-war while Japan was still under the American occupation and has been in force since 1947.

Japan's present-day constitution is comprised of the pre-amble and one hundred and three articles which cover areas such as: the Emperor, the renunciation of war, the rights and duties of the people, the National Diet, the Cabinet, and the administration of justice. The modern Constitution of Japan differs from that of the Meiji Era in that sovereignty rests with the people and not the Emperor, there is a greater emphasis on pacifism and the basic rights of the people are guaranteed.

Basic human rights include, to begin with, freedom of religion, freedom of thought and conscience and freedom of the press and of speech. As well as these, the right of each citizen to demand of the state the ability to lead a reasonable human existence (the 'right to live') and the right to privacy are also covered by such rights.

With the development of computers, the need for a system to protect privacy became apparent and in 1988 the 'law to protect personal information' was promulgated.

### The National Diet

The National Diet is Japan's sole legislative body and is made up of the House of Representatives (the Lower House) and the House of Councilors (the Upper House). The are 480 members of the Lower House and 252 members of the Upper House. The proportion of female representation in the Diet was reported in 2000 as being 10.7% , which when compared with other democracies, ranks lower in the world. It is quite easy to see that men run the politics in Japan.

In 1993, during the time of the Hosokawa Cabinet, a woman, Takako Doi, was elected as the Speaker of the House of Representatives and women were appointed as government ministers. The role of women in Japanese politics began to make a strong impact. It is believed that the numbers of female Diet members will continue to increase in the future.

### Elections

Diet members are elected to their positions by the people. At the time of an election, ballot papers are sent out to every eligible voter over the age of twenty in each city, town and village. When a person reaches the age of twenty-five, they earn the right of elegibility for election.

Members of the Lower House are elect-

衆議院議員の任期は4年ですが、これまでの例では平均2年半で国会が解散し、選挙となっています。参議院議員の任期は6年で、3年ごとに半数が改選されることになっています。

## ●政権交代

1993年に細川政権によって、自民党の40年間に及ぶ1党支配の長期政権が崩れて、日本の政治はこれから連立の時代に向かおうとしています。デモクラシー社会を築くには、1つの思想よりも、もっと多様な価値観や思想が必要なのではないでしょうか。

## ●内閣

中央省庁が2001年1月6日1府12省庁の体制に再編成された。それまで1府22省庁あったことを考えると、かなり大胆な改革である。

改革の特徴は「内閣府」(総理府、経済企画、沖縄開発両庁が母体)が新設されたこと、そして省庁が統合されたことだ。郵政、自治、総務3省庁は「総務省」に、文部省、科学技術庁は「文部科学省」に、厚生、労働両省は「厚生労働省」に、運輸、建設、北海道開発、国土の4省庁は「国土交通省」に統合された。また「環境庁」が「環境省」に「大蔵省」は「財務省」に、「通商産業省」は「経済産業省」に名称を変更した。大改革によって日本の行政が「官僚主導」から「政治主導」に変わるのか、国民の声は行政に届くのか、良い改革であることが望まれている。

## ●裁判所

日本の司法を担当しています。刑事事件と民事事件によって、最高裁判所、高等裁判所、地方裁判所、簡易裁判所へ、あるいは家庭裁判所へ訴えることができます。

しかし、日本はアメリカ社会とは異なり、話し合いで解決できれば裁判するまでもないという考え方が強く、民事の場合は示談ですむことも多いのです。

ed for a term of four years, however, to date there has been a dissolution of the Diet every two and a half years, on average, leading to an election. Members of the Upper House serve a six year term, with an election of half of the members every three years.

**Transfer of Political Power**

In 1993, the Hosokawa Administration ended the long 40 years of single-party rule of the Liberal Democratic Pary, ushering a new era of coalition government into the world of Japanese politics. In order to build a democratic society, it may be necessary to have various ideas and values, rather than a single ideology. Perhaps this might be a way of interpreting these events.

**The Cabinet**

On January 6, 2001, the national government was reorganized into the Cabinet Office and twelve ministries and agencies. This was a rather bold reformation, considering that the prior administrative structure was made up of the Prime Minister's Office and twenty-two ministries and agencies. The major changes accomplished through the reorganization were the establishment of the Cabinet Office (created from mainly the Prime Minister's Office, the Economic Planning Agency, and the Okinawa Development Agency), and the integration of some ministries and agencies into new ministries. The Ministry of Posts and Telecommunications, the Ministry of Home Affairs, and the Management and Coordination Agency were combined to form the Ministry of General Affairs; the Ministry of Education and the Science and Technology Agency became the Ministry of Education, Science and Technology; the Ministry of Health and Welfare and the Ministry of Labor became the Ministry of Labor and Welfare; and the Ministry of Transport, the Ministry of Construction, the Hokkaido Development Agency, and the National Land Agency became the Ministry of National Land and Transport. Additionally, three departments were renamed, with the Environment Agency changing to the Ministry of the Environment, the Ministry of Finance changing to the Ministry of the Treasury, and the Ministry of International Trade and Industry changing to the Ministry of Economy and Industry. It is hoped that this large-scale restructuring will be a positive change, bringing about a government that is led by politicians, not bureaucrats, and is responsive to the voice of the people.

**The Law Courts**

In Japan, the Courts are responsible for the administration of justice. Legal proceedings, whether criminal cases or civil cases, may be sought in the Supreme Court, the High Court, the District Court, the Summary Court or in Family Court.

Japan differs from American society, however, in that, in Japan, people prefer to resolve matters through negotiation without having to take them to court and many civil cases are apparently resolved through private settlement.

# 日本の経済

## The Japanese Economy

日本の経済は、1960年代から何度か不況になりかけながらも、それを乗り越え高い成長を続けてきました。しかし、1991年を頂点に1992年には景気が後退しています。

1992年に経済審議会が出した「生活大国5か年計画」には、次のようなことが書かれています。

「今までは生産力をあげることを重視してきたが、これからは国民1人1人の生活を大切にする」

「日本の経済力を高めることだけを考えるのではなく、地球社会の調和を考える」

1990年代、日本人の「物」に対する満足は得られたと考え、これからは労働時間を短縮したり、余暇を楽しむ生活を実現することをあげているのです。

## ●生活大国5か年計画

この「生活大国5か年計画」には「年間1800時間の労働時間に減らしたい」「大都市に住む人の住宅を年収の5倍で買えるようにしたい」があげられています。

しかし、実現にはむずかしいものがあります。なぜなら、日本は狭い土地に多くの人が住んでいるため、住宅の値段がとても高いからです。

日本人のサラリーマンの働く時間は、通勤時間も含めると1日10時間以上という人は普通で、8時間労働に残業が2時間、通勤距離が往復3時間、1日に13時間も拘束されているという人も珍しくないのです。

今のサラリーマンの暮らしが諸外国とくらべて、どんなに人間らしい生活からかけ離れているかがわかります。

## ●国際化を目指して

「円」や「物」は世界を自由に歩きまわっています。海外旅行するのに、以前はドルを準備しましたが、今は円でたいていの国は大丈夫です。

しかし、日本の文化や習慣となると、お金や物のように

The Japanese economy, while teetering on the verge of recession a number of times during and after the 1960's, managed to ride out these times and continued to sustain high economic growth. This reached a peak in 1991 and in 1992 Japan entered a period of economic slowdown.

In 1992, the Economic Deliberative Council issued its 'Life-style Super Power 5-Year Plan', in which it stated: 'To date, much has been made of raising productivity, however, from now on, there will be greater consideration of the individual needs of the people.'

'Rather than merely considering how to increase Japan's economic strength, more attention is to be paid to the harmony of the global society.'

In the 1990's, a certain degree of satisfaction has been achieved in 'things' Japanese and so, efforts are being made to achieve a better life-style--one in which there is enjoyment of leisure, with a reduction in working hours.

### The Life-Style Super Power Five Year Plan

In the 'Life-style Super Power 5-Year Plan', it has been proposed that 'the number of working hours per year be reduced to 1800 and that people living in large cities be able to buy a residence for the equivalent of 5 times their annual salary.'

However, the realization of such goals is no easy matter. The reason for this is that in Japan, large numbers of people living on a limited amount of land makes for exhorbitant prices in housing.

It is normal for a Japanese office worker to work at least ten hours a day, which would include commuting time and it is not unusual to find people who are actually working as many as thirteen hours a day, when you add two hours of overtime to the eight-hour working day, as well as three hours of commuting time (return trip).

Compared to other foreign contries, it is easy to see how far removed the lifestyle of a Japanese office worker is from that of a decent human-like existence.

### Towards Internationalization

Throughout the world, people have become familiar with the 'yen' and Japanese 'goods'. In the past, when one wished to travel overseas, it was necessary to take American dollars. These days, it is possible to get by with Japanese yen in most countries.

When it comes to the questions of Japanese culture or traditions, one discovers that, unlike Japanese 'currency' and 'goods', these have not been exported to the four corners of the globe, and it seems that efforts need to be made to increase

世界のあちこちに輸出されたわけではなく、世界の人に理解してもらうように努力しなくてはいけないようです。

たとえば、商取引では、輸入を規制したり、外国の企業が入ってこられない仕組みになっていることに批判があります。不必要な規制は早くやめ、市場開放を進めるべきです。日本が一方的に輸出していたのでは、国際収支は黒字が続き、バランスが悪くなるばかりです。

しかし、一番問題になっているのは、商取引の習慣が違うことのようです。どちらか一方の方法が正しく、他方は悪いと決めつけるのではなく、お互いのやり方を理解し合うようにしなくてはいけないと思います。そのためには、留学生や外国人社員をもっと受け入れて日本の習慣を理解してもらうこと、それから日本人も外国人に接して、自分たちとの考えの違いを知る必要があります。

## ●円高

日本の円は1973年に変動相場制になりました。そして、日本は円高がどんどん進んでいます。

その理由は経済成長率が比較的高いこと、物価上昇率が低いこと、そして貿易で黒字が続いていることなどです。

もちろん、その背景には、各国が協調して円高にしようとしたことがあります。

円高の結果、日本の経済は輸出する製品の多い自動車や電気産業が打撃をうけました。輸入物価は下がり、国内に輸入品が増えました。この先も円高は一層進み、日本の経済は試練に立たされていくでしょう。

## ●内需拡大

この言葉には、特別な意味が込められています。それは日本では、海外への輸出が多く、輸入が少ないことから、外国との経済摩擦が起きているからです。特にアメリカからは強い不満が出ています。日本国内での需要をもっと高くする、それが、結果的には外国との輸出と輸入のバランスを保つことができるのです。

international understanding.

For example, in business dealings, the regulation of imports and the existence of mechanisms which make it impossible for foreign corporations to enter Japan have drawn criticism. Unnecessary regulation should be quickly dispensed with and the opening of markets should be accelerated. Japan's history of exporting in a uni-lateral way and always being in the black has led to an ever-worsening imbalance of international payments.

The greatest problems however, seem to derive from the different practises in business dealings. It is not a question of accusing one party of being 'in the right' and the other of being 'in the wrong'--efforts to ensure mutual understanding of the proceedings involved must be pursued by both parties.

To this end, it is necessary to accept foreign students and to employ foreign workers in companies and to have them gain an understanding of Japanese customs--Japanese and foreigners need to interact in order to learn about each other's different viewpoints.

### The Appreciation of the Yen

In 1973 Japan adopted the floating exchange rate system for the yen. Since this time Japan has seen its currency grow from strength to strength.

The strong yen may be attributed to the comparatively high level of economic growth, the slow rise of commodity prices and the fact that trade figures continue to remain in the black. Certainly, the concerted action of many countries to create a stong yen has set the scene for the present situation.

The impact of a strong yen has meant that the Japanese economy has been hit hard--in particular, car manufacturers and the electronics industry, which depend upon large numbers of exports. The prices of inported goods have dropped and the numbers of domestic imports have swelled. With the continued strengthening of the yen, Japan's economy appears to be in for an ordeal.

### The Expansion of Domestic Consumption

This expression has an underlying particular significance. This is to say that, in Japan, because of the large volume of foreign exports and the small volume of imports, a situation of economic friction with foreign countries has come about. The United States, in particular, has expressed a strong sense of dissatisfaction. Increasing Japanese domestic consumption will, in the long run, contribute towards maintaining the balance of foreign imports and exports.

# 日本の産業
## Japanese Industry

高度経済成長により、農業から第2次・第3次産業に移る人が増え、農業人口は急激に減った

▲真珠の養殖。加工され日本の特産品として、世界各国に輸出される

▼電気製品・電子製品の安売り店が集合しているアキハバラの商店街

自動車、電機とともに日本の工業を代表する精密工業——ビデオカメラの生産ライン

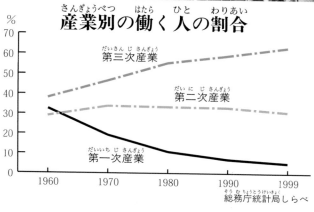

### 産業別の働く人の割合

%

第三次産業

第二次産業

第一次産業

70
60
50
40
30
20
10
0

1960　1970　1980　1990　1999

総務庁統計局しらべ

# 交通と輸送
## Transportation System

大都市間を高速で結ぶ新幹線。常にスピード・アップがはかられている。最新型電車「のぞみ」

都市の近郊を走る電車。通勤・通学や観光地への足になっている

▲空の乗客、貨物も年々増加し、空港の拡張や新設が行われている

路線バスは庶民の足。▶通勤・通学・買い物に多くの人が利用する

◀高速道路と大型トラックで、貨物輸送が便利になった

小さな貨物を扱う宅配▶便は一般家庭の利用で急成長した

# 公害と環境
## Pollution and the Environment

日本は経済の急成長で工業化が進み、各地で環境破壊がおこりました。大気汚染、水や土地の汚れなどによって、大きな被害が出ましたが、今は公害を防止する方法がとられ、環境を保つ努力がされています。環境破壊は地球規模で取り組む時代になっています。

Japan's economic growth resulted in industrial progress, as well as in environmental damage in many areas. A large amount of damage has been caused by air pollution and the contamination of water and soil, but now there are ways to control pollution, and efforts are being made to protect the environment. The time has come to deal with environmental pollution on a local scale.

石油コンビナート（右）や火力発電所（下）も、現在は公害防止の装置がとりつけられ、安全な環境が保てるようになった

### 主な公害発生地域

神通川下流域
（イタイイタイ病）

四日市市
（四日市ぜんそく）

水俣湾沿岸
（水俣病）

東京の町中から出た大量の
ゴミは東京湾の処分場に埋
め立てられる

ゴミを集めて処分場に運ぶ
トラック（清掃車）

燃えるゴミ、燃えないゴミ
を分けてボックスに捨てる

これも公害、放置され
た古タイヤの山

酸性雨で白く立ち枯れ
た木

# 日本の産業

にほん さんぎょう

第１次産業を農業、林業、水産業、第２次産業を鉱業、建設業、製造業、第３次産業を運輸、通信、サービス業とすると、現在の日本で一番多いのは、第３次産業に従事する人たちです。

産業が発展し人びとの収入が増えて、お金の使い方も変わってきました。1970年ごろは、１か月の中で約30パーセントを食費が占めていましたが、1994年には、食費は24%に減り、かわりに教育費、通信費、交通費が増えています。一般に消費支出の中で、食費のしめる割合が小さいほど生活は豊かだと言われています。第３次産業が増えたことと、お金の使い方が変わってきたのは、関係があるようです。

産業のありかたが変わったのは1960年代の高度成長からで、農業や漁業で働く若者たちが、都会に出て働くようになったのです。

国内総生産高にも、産業の変化の様子がはっきり表れています。1970年には第１次産業が4.5兆円、第２次産業が32.7兆円、第３次産業が38.6兆円でした。

しかし1990年代には、第１次産業の生産高が約10兆円にしかならなかったのに対して、第３次産業は254兆円にもなっています。ここからも日本の社会の変化を見てとることができます。

貿易という点を考えると、これからの日本の産業は世界との協力を考えていかなくてはなりません。現地企業との技術提携をすること、現地企業との合弁企業を作り、組み立てや生産を現地ですることなどによって、貿易の上での輸出入もバランスのとれたものとなっていきます。

発展途上国が工業化するための政策的な産業を援助すること、そうすることによって現地の働く人たちの雇用の機会も増やすことができます。それが日本の利潤のためではなく、長期的に現地の人びとのためになるように貢献することが、これからの日本の産業の課題でしょう。

## Japanese Industry

Primary industries include agriculture, forestry and the marine product industry. Secondary industries comprise mining, the construction industry and the manufacturing industry. Tertiary industries cover the transportation, communication and service industries and it is this third sector which employs the largest number of people, in modern-day Japan.

With the development of industry, people's incomes have increased and with this, the way people spend money has also changed. In the early 1970's, approximately thirty per cent of people's monthly salaries was spent on food. In 1994, this figure had dropped to 24%, while the amounts spent on education, communication and transport had increased. Generally speaking, in terms of consumption and expenditure, the less money spent on food, the more affluent the life-style, or so it is said. It would seem that there is some connection between the fact that the tertiary industry sector has grown and the fact that people are spending money differently.

The nature of industry began to undergo a change in the 1960's, during Japan's rapid economic growth period, due to numbers of young people engaged in agriculture and the fishing industries moving to the cities for work.

The change in the situation with industries is clearly reflected in the gross domestic output, as well. In 1970, the figures for primary industries were 4.5 trillion yen, for secondary industries, 32.7 trillion yen and for the tertiary industries 38.6 trillion yen. However, in the early 1990's, primary industries marked an output of only 10 trillion yen, while the teritiary industries attained an output of as much as 254 trillion yen. Through such phenomena, it is also possible to make observations of the changes in Japanese society.

When looking at the question of trade, Japanese industry is going to have to give serious consideration to colaborating on a global scale.

By engaging in technical co-operation with local enterprises, by creating joint ventures with local firms and by having product assembly and production carried out locally, the balance of trade, and moreover that of imports and exports, will be maintained.

By supporting productive industries contributing to the industrialization of developing countries, more opportunities of employment for local workers will be provided. Such efforts are not to be regarded as a source of profit for Japan--the assignment of Japanese industry is to make a long-lasting contribution to the lives of the local people.

# 交通と輸送

## ■鉄道

　日本の鉄道は1872年に開通しました。国が経営する国鉄として1987年まで114年間、日本の鉄道の中心になったきました。その後国鉄は民営化され、現在は、ＪＲ東日本、ＪＲ東海、ＪＲ西日本など６つの旅客会社と、貨物鉄道会社に分けられています。ＪＲの１日の利用客数は、一番多い新宿駅では151万人にもなります。東京圏や京阪神地区では、私鉄の交通網も発達しています。大都市の地下を走る地下鉄も年々のびています。ＪＲは新幹線をふくめ約２万キロ、私鉄は6600キロが日本の国土を走っています。

## ■バス・トラック

　日本の道路は、国道の舗装率は100％に近く、一般道路も舗装されているところが多く、車にとっては便利になりました。バス路線も全国に広がっています。鉄道よりも料金が安いことで地方に行く高速バスの利用者も増えています。お座敷を備え、カラオケを楽しみながら移動する豪華バスも出現し、社員旅行などにも利用されています。
　貨物輸送も鉄道から今ではほとんど自動車になりました。生産地と消費地の間を昼夜を問わず大型トラックが走っています。また、小さな荷物を扱う宅配便は、早くて安全なので、一般消費者には大いに利用されています。

## ■飛行機

　東京から大阪に行く場合、飛行機にしようか新幹線にしようか迷います。時間も料金もほとんど変わらないからです。しかし他の地方に行く場合には、料金が高くても時間が節約できる飛行機を選ぶか、時間がかかっても車窓の風景を楽しめる列車で行くかの選択になります。
　空港は日本全国にあり、主な航空会社は日本航空、全日本空輸、日本エアシステム、南西航空、エアー日本などです。航空機の数も各社を合わせると約300機で国際線と合わせると、日本の空もラッシュ状態です。1994年に、初の海上空港として、関西国際空港が開港しました。

## Transportation System

### Railways

The railways were formally opened in Japan in 1872. Japanese National Railways (**Kokutetsu**) which were operated by the government for 114 years until 1987 formed the nucleus of railway operations in Japan. After this, **Kokutetsu** was privatized and is presently divided into six separate railway companies, including both passenger and freight carrying companies. These include The Eastern Japan (JR East), the Central (JR Tokai) and the Western Japan (JR West) Railway Companies.

The number of passengers that use JR East daily at Shinjuku Station, which enjoys the largest crowds, is reported at 1,510,000 people. The traffic network of private railways in the Tokyo area and the Kyoto-Osaka-Kobe regions, is also highly developed. In addition to this, the underground network of subway systems in large cities continues to expand annually. JR has twenty thousand kilometres of lines, including **Shinkansen** ('Super Express') tracks while private railways boast 6,600 kilometres of track, which run the length of the country.

### Buses and Trucks

Of Japan's roads, almost 100 per cent of National highways are surfaced and many ordinary roads are also paved--a convenient situation for cars. The entire nation is also criss-crossed by a network of bus routes. Since it is cheaper to use buses than to go by train, there are growing numbers of people using express bus services to travel to the country. Luxury coaches have appeared, some of which are equipped with rooms, allowing people to travel in comfort, while enjoying **Karaoke**, for example, at the same time. These buses are proving popular for company trips.

Up until thirty years ago the majority of freight was carried by railroad, but these days most freight is sent by road. Large trucks travel between producing districts and consuming areas, day and night. Furthermore, since express freight carriers handling small parcels are able to reach destinations quickly, they provide a service that the average consumer finds he cannot be without.

### Airlines

When travelling from Tokyo to Osaka these days, one is in two minds about which option to take--whether to fly or to take the **Shinkansen** ('Super Express'). This is because there is little difference in the amount of time it takes and the fare is much the same. However, when travelling to destinations further afield, one is faced with the choice of catching a plane which is more expensive but saves on time, or going by train, which takes longer, but allows a person the opportunity to enjoy the scenery from the train window.

There are airports located throughout Japan, these days. The main airline companies include Japan Airlines, All-Nippon Airways, Japan Air Systems, South-West Airlines and Air Nippon, among others. The combined total number of aircraft comes to approximately three hundred planes, meaning that, when one takes into consideration the addition of international routes, the skies over Japan are heavily congested. In 1994, the world's first airport, completely surrounded by water was opened--the Kansai International Airport.

# 公害と環境

## Pollution and the Environment

日本が高度成長期にあった1960年代、工業化が進展するにつれて各地にさまざまな公害問題が起きました。

その中でも代表的なものが、水俣病、四日市ぜんそく、イタイイタイ病などです。

水俣病は熊本県の水俣湾周辺で発生した、工場排水の有機水銀による中毒症です。水俣湾でとれた魚を食べた人の神経がおかされ、手や足が麻痺したり、言語障害がおきて話もできなくなります。1992年までに2946人の人が水俣病と認定され、その内約半数の人が苦しみながら亡くなっています。1964年には同じ有機水銀による中毒が、新潟県で発生しました（第二水俣病）。カナダでも水俣病が発見されています。

イタイイタイ病は富山県神通川流域に発生した奇病で、身体中の骨がゆがんだり、ひびが入ったりします。患者が「痛い痛い」と苦痛を訴え続けたところから付けられた名前です。原因は神通川の上流にある工場から流れ出た毒が農地を汚染し、カドミウム中毒を起こしたのです。

四日市ぜんそくは大気汚染による公害の一つです。日本で一番大きい石油コンビナートは、1959年に三重県の四日市市で操業を始めました。煙突からでる煙は高度成長のシンボルでした。しかし煙に大量の硫黄酸化物が含まれていて、多くの市民がぜんそくに苦しんだのです。

### ●工業と環境の両立

四日市の場合、裁判で企業の責任が全面的に認められました。これは「経済大国」から「公害大国」になってしまった日本に対する良い警告になりました。

その後、四日市は大気汚染防止に取り組み始めました。1990年には「国際環境技術移転センター」が作られ、四日市での公害防止の方法を発展途上国に伝えることにしたのです。今までに中国、ポーランドなど16か国から研修生がおとずれているそうです。

## Pollution and the Environment

In the 1960's, when Japan was experiencing a period of rapid economic growth, the spread of industrialization gave rise to numerous problems of environmental pollution throughout the country. Typical of these were: 'Minamata Disease', 'Yokkaichi Asthma' and 'Itai Itai ('Ouch, Ouch') Disease'.

Minamata Disease, a kind of industrial poisoning caused by organic mercury, occurred in the Minamata Bay area of Kumamoto Prefecture. People who had eaten fish caught in Minamata Bay suffered paralysis to the arms and legs, as the nerves were affected. They also suffered speech impediments leading to the loss of the ability to talk. To the year 1992, 2,946 cases of Minamata Disease have been acknowledged, with approximately half of these people having experienced a painful death. In 1964, a similar case of organic mercury poisoning was reported in Niigata Prefecture (referred to as 'Minamata Disease No 2'). Reports of an outbreak of Minamata Disease in Canada are also on record.

Itai, Itai ('Ouch, Ouch') Disease occurred around the basin of the Jintsu River in Toyama Prefecture. People with this strange disease suffered bending and cracking of the bones. This disease was given the name Itai Itai because of patients complaining of the pain, 'Ouch, Ouch!'. The cause of this disease has been determined to be cadmium poisoning, resulting from the contamination of farmland due to industrial poisons being released from factories in the upper reaches of the Jintsu River.

Yokkaichi Asthma is a complaint caused by environmental pollution, more specifically air pollution. In 1959, Japan's largest petroleum complex began operating in Yokkaichi City, Mie Prefecture. Smoke belching from chimneys symbolized Japan's rapid economic growth. However, the smoke contained large amounts of sulphur oxide, resulting in many asthma cases among citizens.

### The Co-Existence of Manufacturing Industries and the Environment

In the Yokkaichi case, the Court found the Company concerned to be solely responsible. This served as a warning to Japan--a nation that, from being an 'Economic Superpower', had become a 'Polluting Superpower'.

After this case, Yokkaichi City set about grappling with the prevention of air pollution. In 1990 the 'International Centre for the Transfer of Environmental Technology' was established and it was decided that methods employed in the prevention of environmental pollution in Yokkaichi City would be promoted in the developing countries. To date, research trainees from sixteen countries, including China and Poland have visited the Centre.

北九州市も「公害」から「環境」へと生まれ変わった都市です。1960年代、北九州市はたくさんの煙突から酸化鉄を含んだ赤い煙や煤煙の黒い煙など、「七色」の煙が出て、スモッグの街でした。海の汚染もひどく、沿岸の工場から排水が流れ込み、魚も住めない「死の海」でした。1971年、北九州市は「公害防止条例」を出し、工場に排水浄化施設や煙から硫黄をとりのぞく装置をつけるように指導しました。

今では、かつての「死の海」に115種類もの魚や貝が住むようになりました。これからは、公害防止の経験を世界に伝えようと、1992年に「KITA環境協力センター」が誕生し、インドネシアやアフリカに技術指導や援助を行っています。1992年には「地球サミット」でも表彰されました。これからも「公害」の経験を、教訓として世界に伝えていって欲しいものです。

## ●汚染は地球規模に

世界の各地でも公害問題が発生し、地球全体の汚染や環境破壊はとても深刻な問題です。地球の温暖化、フロンガスによるオゾン層の破壊、熱帯林の急激な減少、森林を枯らす酸性雨、化学物質による海洋汚染などです。

自然環境の中では、植物も動物も、お互いに影響を与えながら生態系をつくっています。しかし、公害や環境破壊によって、動物や植物ばかりではなく、気象、土壌、地形なども影響を受けるのです。人間の利害だけではなく、生態系全体のことを考えなければいけない時期にきているようです。

## ●ゴミ

一般家庭から出るゴミが年間1億トン、産業廃棄物が2億トン、日本の沿岸部はこれらのゴミで埋め立てられてきました。しかし、もう場所がありません。これらのゴミの中身を見ると、半分は再利用できるものが多いのです。分けて捨てること、作る人が捨てる費用を考えて作ることを心がければ、ゴミはもっと減るに違いありません。

Kitakyushu City has also undergone a 'reincarnation'--from being a city associated with pollution, to being one conscious of the environment. In the 1960's Kitakyushu City was known as a city of smog. With red smoke, containing iron oxide and black sooty smoke belching from its many smoke-stacks, it was a city 'renowned' for its many varieties of coloured smoke. The sea was badly polluted with factories located along the coast releasing industrial waste, making the sea unfit for fish to live in--a 'sea of death', in fact. In 1971, Kitakyushu City announced regulations for the prevention of environmental pollution and directed factories to install waste purification equipment and devices to remove sulphur from industrial smoke.

Today, 115 different varieties of fish and shellfish survive in the 'sea of death'. In 1992, the KITA Environmental Co-operation Centre was established, with the aim of sharing its experience of pollution control with the world. The Centre has sent teams to Indonesia and Africa with technical advice and assistance. At the 1992 'Earth Summit', the Centre received an official commendation. May the lessons learned from these experiences of environmental pollution be made known to the rest of the world.

**Pollution on a Global Scale**

Problems involving environmental pollution have occurred throughout the world--pollution and destruction of the environment on a global scale are serious matters, indeed. These problems include: global warming, the destruction of the Ozone layer caused by flurocarbons, the rapid reduction of tropical rainforest areas, the devastation of forests due to acid rain and sea pollution caused by chemical substances.

In the natural environment, plants and animals interact with each other, creating the ecosystem. However, due to the influence of pollution and disruption of the environment, it is not only plants and animals that are affected--weather conditions, the soil and topography are also influenced. It is not merely for the interests of mankind, but for the sake of the whole of the ecosystem that the time has come for us to address this situation.

**Garbage**

The amount of garbage generated by average families in Japan every year amounts to 100 million tons, while industrial waste accounts for 200 million tons. To date, this garbage has been used as landfill in Japan's coastal areas. However, there is no more space to dispose of the garbage. When we examine the contents of the garbage, we find that half of it is, in fact, recyclable. If we were to set our minds on taking steps such as separating the garbage when we dispose of it, or having the manufacturers of products consider the costs of disposal in the manufacturing process, the amount of garbage could surely be reduced.

# 日本の歴史
## Japanese History

日本が国として成立したのは、4世紀の大和政権からです。いらい約1700年、日本人の生活・文化、外国との交流、戦争、さまざまの出来事をおりまぜた中に、現在の日本があります。ここでは日本の歴史を一通り時代の流れにそって見ていくことにします。

The Japanese nation began with the foundation of the Yamato state in the fourth century. Since then, almost 1,700 years of Japanese life and culture, foreign relations and wars has produced today's Japan. Here, we will look over Japan's history through the flow of the centuries.

# 日 本 の 歴 史 年 表

| 区分 | 年代 | |
|---|---|---|
| 旧石器時代 | B.C. 8000 | |
| 縄文時代 | | 縄文文化 |
| | B.C. 300 | 弥生文化 |
| 弥生時代 | | 女王卑弥呼（邪馬台国） |
| | A.D. 300 | 大和政権誕生 |
| 大和時代 | 500 | 中国から漢字が伝わる |
| | 600 | 聖徳太子、国政を担当<br>17条の憲法を定める<br>中国から仏教が伝わる<br>法隆寺が建てられる |
| 奈良時代 | | |

縄文式土器

弥生式土器

法隆寺（世界最古の木造建築）

93

| | | | |
|---|---|---|---|
| 奈良時代 | 710 | 奈良に都をさだめる<br>（平城京）<br><br>律令体制できる<br><br>『万葉集』 | |
| 平安時代 | 794 | 京都に都をさだめる<br>（平安京）<br><br>貴族文化が盛ん<br>『枕草子』『源氏物語』<br><br>武士が育つ（平氏と源氏が有力） | <br>源氏物語絵巻 |
| 鎌倉時代 | 1185<br>1192<br><br>1274<br>1281 | 源氏が平氏を滅ぼす<br>源頼朝、鎌倉に幕府を開く<br><br>元が二度にわたって攻めてくる（文永の役・弘安の役） | <br>文永の役（元との戦い） |
| 室町時代 | 1333<br><br>1467<br><br>1543 | 鎌倉幕府が滅びる<br><br>応仁の乱<br><br>ポルトガルから鉄砲伝わる | <br>鎌倉時代の武士 |

| | | | |
|---|---|---|---|
| 安土・桃山時代 | 1549 | 信長、天下統一にのりだす |  |
| | | ザビエルがキリスト教を伝える | |
| | 1590 | 秀吉、天下を統一する | |
| | | 「検地」や「刀狩り」が行われる | |

織田信長　　豊臣秀吉　　徳川家康

| | | | |
|---|---|---|---|
| 江戸時代 | 1600 | 関ヶ原の戦い |  |
| | 1603 | 家康、江戸に幕府を開く | |
| | | 「参勤交代」制度 | |
| | 1639 | 鎖国が完成 | |

姫路城（法隆寺と共に世界の文化遺産）

| | | |
|---|---|---|
| | | 井原西鶴『日本永代蔵』 |
| | | 町人文化が栄える（歌舞伎・浮世絵） |

参府行列図（大名行列）

| | | |
|---|---|---|
| | 1853 | ペリーが浦賀にくる |
| | 1867 | 徳川15代将軍が政権を天皇にかえす |

浮世絵「東海道五十三次・日本橋」

| | | |
|---|---|---|
| 明治時代 | 1868 | 明治維新 |
| | 1864 | 首都を東京にさだめる |
| | 1871 | 「廃藩置県」 |
| | 1889 | 大日本帝国憲法を発布 |
| | 1894 | 日清戦争 |
| | 1904 | 日露戦争 |

明治初期に品川海岸を走る汽車

| | | |
|---|---|---|
| 大正時代 | 1914 | 第一次世界大戦 |
| | 1923 | 関東大震災 |
| 昭和時代 | 1931 | 満洲事変 |
| | 1937 | 日中戦争 |
| | 1941 | 太平洋戦争 |
| | 1945 | 広島・長崎に原子爆弾が落とされる |
| | | ポツダム宣言を受ける |
| | 1946 | 日本国憲法を公布 |
| | | 戦後の大改革 |
| | 1964 | 東京(夏季)オリンピック |
| | 1968 | 川端康成、ノーベル文学賞を受賞 |
| | 1970 | 日本万国博覧会 |
| 平成時代 | 1994 | 大江健三郎、ノーベル文学賞を受賞 |
| | 1995 | 阪神・淡路大震災 |
| | 1998 | 長野(冬季)オリンピック |

東京オリンピック

大震災で横倒しになった
阪神高速道路(1995)

海から見た東京の夜景

# 日本の歴史

## ●原始社会から古代社会へ

今から13万年前から1万年前までの約12万年は、狩猟、採集を中心に家族単位で暮らした石器時代です。

紀元前8000年から紀元前300年くらいが「縄文文化」の時代です。今も日本の各地から縄の模様のついた土器が発掘されています。「弥生土器」は高温で焼かれた薄手の土器で、稲の跡が発見されたことから、すでに集団による農耕作業があったと言われています。「弥生時代」は紀元前300年くらいに始まり約600年続きます。縄文文化と弥生文化は全く異なった文化を持つ人たちによるものだと言われ、日本人のルーツをさぐる上でも、今も歴史学者たちの関心をひきつけています。

3世紀に中国で書かれた日本に関する文献である『魏志倭人伝』には、「日本には耶馬台国があり、女王である卑弥呼が、民衆を支配している」と書かれています。しかし日本には当時文字もなく、耶馬台国がどこにあったのかも学者によって意見が別れています。

大和政権が誕生したのは3世紀から4世紀の初めです。日本には固有の文字がなく、5世紀前後に中国から漢字が伝わりました。7世紀になると聖徳太子が国政を担当し、隋（中国581～618）と国交を開始したり、17条の憲法を定めたりします。中国から仏教が伝わり、日本の各地に寺院が建てられたり、仏像がつくられたのはこの頃です。

7世紀の中頃には、人民を統一的に政府が支配する律令（政治の基本になる法律）ができ、この律令体制は9世紀（平安時代の初期）まで続きますが、荘園（私有地）を持った貴族社会の出現でそれはこわれていきます。

平安時代（794年から1192年まで）は平安京（今の京都）を中心に貴族文化が花開いた時代です。『源氏物語』『枕草子』などの女流文学や貴族たちの日常生活を記した日記、貴族の家のふすまや屏風にかかれた大和絵からも、その当時の生活をしのぶことができます。

## From Primitive to Ancient Times

From 130,000 years ago to 10,000 years ago, for approximately 120,000 years during what is known as the Stone Age, there existed a society of mostly hunters and gatherers, living together in family units.

The Jomon Period of history was from 8,000 years BC to about the year 300 BC. Still today, pieces of earthenware with straw rope patterns, known as Jomon-ware, are being unearthed in all parts of the country. From traces of rice plants discovered in Yayoi-ware, eggshell-thin earthenware fired at high temperatures, it has been revealed that communities of people at this time were already involved in agricultural work. The Yayoi Period began in about the year 300 BC and continued for six hundred years. The Jomon and Yayoi cultures are said to be associated with peoples of completely different cultural backgrounds and, in terms of the search for the 'roots' of the Japanese people, they continue to fascinate historians to the present day.

In the **Wajinden** section of the 'Wei Chronicle'--documentary records on Japan, written in the third century in China, it is stated 'In Japan, in the place known as **Yamatai-koku**, Himiko rules her people as queen'. However, since there was no written form of the language in Japan at this time, experts are divided in their opinions as to the whereabouts of Yamatai-koku.

The Yamato Government came into power in the period from about the late third century, to the early fourth century. There was no indigenous writing system in Japan, so **kanji** ('Chinese characters') were introduced from China in about the 5th century. In the 7th Century, Shotoku Taishi assumed the reigns of government. He established diplomatic relations with the **Sui** Dynasty in China (581-618 AD) and promulgated the 'Constitution of Seventeen Articles'. Buddhism was introduced from China and temples were built throughout the country--Buddhist images began to be created from this time.

Around the middle of the 7th Century, a series of statutes (laws forming the foundation of government) were introduced by the government in an attempt to bring the poeople under a single authority. This system of statutes remained in force until the 9th Century (the beginning of the Heian Period), but broke down with the emergence of the aristocratic classes, who possessed manors and private land.

The Heian Period (from the year 794 to the year 1192), with its administrative centre in Heiankyo (present-day Kyoto) was a time when the aristocracy was in its heyday. 'Works of female literature' such as 'The Tale of Genji' and 'The Pillow Book of Sei Shonagon', the diaries of aristocrats containing descriptions of everyday life and Yamato-e pictures painted on sliding and folding screens from the houses of noblemen help to remind us of these times.

## ●封建社会前期（鎌倉・室町・安土／桃山）

　平安時代の中頃から農業生産力の上昇によって有力者が出現し、武士が育っていきます。その中でも平氏と源氏が最も有力でしたが、1185年「壇の浦の合戦」で源氏が平氏を滅ぼし、1192年 源 頼朝が鎌倉に幕府を開きます。江戸時代まで約700年間続く、武家政治の始まりです。

　源 頼朝は鎌倉を根拠地にして、各地に守護と地頭をおいて、支配力を全国に広げていきました。守護は軍事と警察、そして地頭はその年の年貢（農民に課す税）を取り立てる役目がありました。

　源氏の将軍は３代で絶え、その後北条氏が執権という幕府の要職についている時、京都の朝廷との間で戦いがありました。この時は幕府軍は朝廷軍を破りましたが、二度にわたる元（中国の国名）のフビライハンとの戦い（1274年約４万人の大軍、1281年朝鮮人も動員した14万人の大軍が攻めてきた）で、幕府の力は弱まりました。御家人（家来の武士）たちはよろい、かぶと、武器、馬などを用意したり兵士をやとったりして、たくさんの出費がありましたが、幕府からは何の恩賞もなく、不満を持つ武士が増えていったのです。天皇はそれらの武士たちの力を借りて鎌倉幕府を滅ぼし、朝廷を中心とした政治を始めました。

　しかしこれも一時的なもので、武士の足利氏を中心とした室町幕府が再び京都につくられ、240年間も続きます。この時代は貴族や僧侶、武士の間だけでなく民衆の間にも文化が広まりました。能や狂言が育ち、京都では絹織物の西陣織や刀造りなどの手工業が発達しました。この時代には瀬戸内海や日本海沿岸にも港町が栄え、決まった日に市が開かれ、さまざまなものが売り買いされました。

　室町時代の中頃、将軍の跡継ぎをめぐって「応仁の乱」が起き、その後日本の各地で実力のある大名どうしが争って戦乱が100 年間も続きます。織田信長は、合戦に初めてポルトガルから伝わった鉄砲を使い、天下を統一したのです。1549年、フランシスコ・ザビエルによってキリスト教が伝わり、信長はキリスト教を保護しました。

## The Age of Feudalism
### First Half (Kamakura, Muromachi and Azuchi/Momoyama Periods)

From the middle of the Heian Period, with the increase in agricultural output, there emerged influential people and in turn, the samurai warrior class began to thrive. Of these influential groups, the Heishi and Genji families were the most powerful and in 1185, at the 'Battle of Dan no Ura', the Genji clan overthrew the Heishi Clan. In 1192, Minamoto-no-Yoritomo became Shogun and established his shogunate in Kamakura. This heralded a period of 700 years of military rule until the Edo Period.

Minamoto-no-Yoritomo set up a stronghold in Kamakura, established defences and installed a 'Lord of the Manor' in each region, allowing him to assume control over the whole country. The defences included military forces and police. The function of the Lord of the Manor was to collect the land taxes (imposed on the peasants) each year.

The Shoguns of the Genji clan continued for three generations. After this, while Hojo was installed as shikken ('regent'--an important post as advisor to the Shogun), a battle was fought with the Kyoto Imperial court forces. The Shogunate troops defeated the Imperial troops on this occasion. On two further occasions, however, battles were fought with Kublai Khan and his army from Gen (a Mongolian country)--first in 1274, the Mongolian forces attacked with a large army, 40,000 strong and then again in 1281, when a huge army of 140,000, including men mobilized from Korea, launched an attack. These battles left the Kamakura Shogunate in a weakened state. Samurai warriors who were vassals to the Shogun had large outlays of expense--readying armor, helmets, weapons and horses, as well as employing soldiers. Since they didn't feel that they were receiving any benefit from the shogunate the number of disgruntled samurai warriors grew. The Emperor, using these samurai to his advantage, overthrew the Kamakura Shogunate and installed an imperial court centralized government.

However, this too, was short-lived when the military Commander Ashikaga established the Muromachi shogunate, once again in Kyoto. This period of history continued for 240 years, during which time there was great cultural development, not merely among the ranks of the aristocracy and Buddhist priests, but also among the people in general. Noh and Kyogen theatre flourished and in Kyoto, handicrafts such as Nishijin silk brocade and sword making developed. This time also saw port towns along the Inland Sea and on the Sea of Japan coast thrive--markets were held on appointed days with goods of all varieties being bought and sold.

Towards the middle of the Muromachi period, due to a struggle among possible successors to the Shogun, the 'Battle of Onin' broke out. This, in turn, led to a period of 100 years of war with powerful daimyo, or feudal lords throughout Japan, fighting against each other. Oda Nobunaga, using guns introduced from Portugal in battle for the first time, managed to unify the whole country. In 1549, St Francis Xavier brought Christianity to Japan and this new religion was protected by Nobunaga.

## ●封建社会後期（安土／桃山・江戸）

　信長が殺された後、天下を統一したのは豊臣秀吉です。秀吉は大阪城をつくり、城下には多くの家来、商人、職人を集めました。その結果大阪は大きな城下町となり商工業が栄えました。農民は「検地」によって田畑の面積を調べて年貢が決められ、「刀狩り」で刀、やり、鉄砲などすべての武器をとりあげられ、村を離れたり身分を変えることができなくなりました。秀吉はキリスト教を弾圧し、また二度も朝鮮を侵略しようとしましたが、この戦いの途中で死にました。

　秀吉の死後、徳川家康が「関が原の戦い（1600年）」に勝って政権をにぎります。家康は江戸（今の東京）に江戸城をつくらせ、諸国の260あまりの大名の妻子を江戸に住まわせました。大名は「参勤交代」といって1年ごとに江戸と領地に住み、その往復の大名行列（図参照）には、多額の費用が必要でした。幕府は大名に多額の金を使わせ、財力を弱めるようにしたのです。この時代、日本の商人たちは幕府から許可をもらった「朱印船」に乗り、東南アジアの国々にでかけました。外国との貿易が盛んになると、キリスト教の信者も増え、幕府はキリスト教が政治を乱すのではないかと恐れた結果、キリスト教の弾圧が激しくなり鎖国にまで発展しました。日本人や日本船が外国に行くことや、外国から戻ることを禁止したのです。

　大阪は江戸時代も日本一の商業都市として栄えました。井原西鶴（1642—93）の『日本永代蔵』には、船で米が運ばれる様子や、「数千軒の問屋が軒をならべ」とにぎわう様子が描かれています。

　江戸時代は士（武士）農（農民）工（職人）商（商人）の身分がはっきりしていました。武士だけが名字（姓）を名乗り両刀を差す特権を持っていたのです。

　この時代は町人文化が栄え、歌舞伎や人形芝居を人びとは楽しみ、浮世絵も生まれました。

　1853年、浦賀にペリーが率いるアメリカ合衆国の軍艦が現れ、200年も続いた鎖国は終わることになったのです。

## The Age of Feudalism

### The Latter Half (Azuchi/Momoyama, Edo)

After **Nobunaga** was murdered, **Toyotomi Hideyoshi** succeeded as Shogun and reunified the country. **Hideyoshi** built Osaka Castle. Large numbers of vassals, merchants and craftsmen flocked to the castle town, with the result that Osaka became a large centre where commerce and industry flourished. Peasants paid land taxes according to the area of their fields under a land surveying system known as **kenchi**. The non-samurai classes were deprived of all arms, such as swords, spears, firearms and so on, under the **katana-gari** law, meaning that it became impossible for people to leave the village or effect a change in social position. Hideyoshi suppressed Christianity and attempted to invade the Korean Peninsula on two occasions, however he perished in the process.

With the death of Hideyoshi, **Tokugawa Ieyasu** seized power after gaining victory at the Battle of **Sekigahara** in the year 1600. Ieyasu had Edo Castle constructed in Edo (present-day Tokyo) and relocated the wives and family of the **daimyo** of more than 260 different provinces here. The **daimyo** alternated residences between Edo and their fiefs on a yearly basis under a system known as **sankin kotai**. This procession of daimyo, both ways, required huge outlays of funds. (Refer to diagram.) The Shogunate required the **daimyo** to spend vast sums of money, causing their financial resources to be depleted. During this time, Japanese merchants travelled to the countries of South-East Asia on special trading ships authorized by the shogunate. Trade with foreign countries prospered and with this, the number of converts to Christianity also grew. Fearing that Christianity would throw the government into a state of disorder, the shogunate increased suppression of this religion, which inevitably led to the complete isolation of the country. Japanese people and ships were forbidden to travel abroad and likewise, were unable to return from the outside world.

During the Edo Period, Osaka flourished as the number one centre of commerce in Japan. Ihara Saikaku's work **Nihon Eitaigura**, describes lively scenes of ships transporting loads of rice and thousands of wholesale rice stores lining the waterfront.

Social status in the Edo Period was clearly defined--people were classed as **shi** ('warrior'), **no** ('farmer'), **ko** ('artisan'), or **sho** ('tradesman'). Only samurai were allowed the privilege of having a family name and that of wearing two swords.

During this period of history the merchant classes thrived, **Kabuki** theatre and puppet plays enjoyed wide popularity and woodblock prints of the **ukiyoe** ('transitory world painting') style appeared for the first time.

In 1853, American warships, commanded by Commodore Perry, arrived in Uraga, bringing to an end the two hundred years of national isolation.

# ●近代社会（明治・大正・昭和）

　徳川15代将軍の時、政権は天皇にかえり、鎌倉幕府が開かれてから700年続いた武士の時代は終わりました。

　江戸を東京とし、年号も明治としました。1871年には藩を廃止して県とし（「廃藩置県」）、県には政府の任命した知事を派遣しました。これまでの身分制度であった士農工商をなくして、国民は誰でも平等であるとしました。これで、平民（農工商）の人たちも名字を持ち、職業や住むところも自由に選べるようになりました。

　政府ははやく外国に追いつこうと、近代産業をおこすために各地に工場を造ったり、強い軍隊をつくるために徴兵制度を行います。このための費用は税金です。国民には兵役と納税の義務ができました。

　1894年、日本は朝鮮の支配権を得るために、中国と戦争をおこし（日清戦争）、1904年には中国東北部をめぐってロシアと対立し、戦うことになります（日露戦争）。日露戦争の後、日本は朝鮮を併合し植民地としました。やがて軍人が実権をにぎるようになり、日本は軍国主義の道を進んでいきます。1931年、日本軍は満州を攻撃し15年にわたる日中戦争がはじまります。日本は中国侵略やその後のインドシナへの進出でアメリカやイギリスと対立するようになり、1941年、太平洋戦争に突入しました。第2次世界大戦です。1945年、アメリカ軍によって広島と長崎に原爆が投下され、日本政府は連合国側のポツダム宣言を受け入れて降伏しました。原爆によっていまも後遺症に苦しんでいる人たちがいます。こういうことは今後絶対にあってはならないことです。

　戦後、日本は民主国家として生まれ変わりました。それまでの「大日本帝国憲法」にかわる「日本国憲法」ができました。国民主権、基本的人権の尊重、平和主義をかかげた、今までにない新しい憲法です。

　これからは、日本のことだけを考えるのではなく、世界の国々と助け合っていく時代です。もう決して侵略戦争を起こさないためにも。

# The Modern Age

## (Meiji, Taisho and Showa Periods)

　The fifteenth Shogun of the Tokugawa Shogunate, Tokugawa Yoshinobu, handed over government control to the Emperor Meiji, thus bringing to an end the age of the samurai warriors, which had continued for seven hundred years from the time of the Kamakura shogunate.

　Edo assumed the name of Tokyo and the new era was named Meiji. In 1871, feudal clans were abolished and prefectures established (referred to as haihan-chiken). Governors appointed by the government were dispatched to prefectures. The class system, consisting of warriors, farmers, artisans and tradesmen, which had previously existed, was done away with, all citizens being made equal. Thus, the common people, namely farmers, artisans and tradesmen adopted family names and were able to freely choose occupations and where they might live.

　The government, in an attempt to catch up with foreign countries, had factories built throughout the country to boost the development of modern industry. To increase the strength of the military, a conscription system was introduced. To cover the costs of such efforts, compulsory systems of military service and the payment of taxes were imposed on the people.

　In 1894, in an effort to gain control of the Korean Peninsuala, Japan went to war with China (the Sino-Japanese War) and then again, in 1904, launched a military campaign against Russian forces in North-Eastern China (the Russo-Japanese War). After the Russo-Japanese War, Korea was annexed and became a colony of Japan. Finally, the military had a firm grasp on real power, allowing Japan to advance down the road of militarism. In 1931, Japanese forces launched an attack on Manchuria entering a Sino-Japanese conflict which continued for 15 years. With its invasion of China and advance into Indo-China, Japan entered into conflict with the United States and its allies, rushing headlong into the Pacific War, which was to become the Second World War. After atomic bombs were dropped on Hiroshima and Nagasaki by the American forces, the Japanese government accepted the Potsdam Declaration, formulated by the Allied Powers and surrendered. Even today there are people who are suffering from the after-effects of radiation sickness--victims of the atom bombs. This experience must never be allowed to recur.

　After the war, Japan was regenerated as a democratic nation. Under the direction of the General Headquarters of the Allied Forces, the Imperial Constitution or 'the Constitution of the Empire of Japan' was replaced by 'the Constitution of Japan'--a new constitution espousing democratic rights, respect for basic human rights and pacifism.

　The time for co-operation with the nations of the world has arrived--Japan must cease to be 'inward-looking'. In this way, may wars of aggression be only ever things of the past.

## ●掲載写真

| | 〈写 真 内 容〉 | 〈提 供 先〉 |
|---|---|---|
| 日 本 人 の 生 活 | ・公団住宅 | 住宅・都市整備公団 |
| 年 中 行 事 | ・初もうで<br>・おせち料理<br>・節分式<br>・ひな流し<br>・ひな人形<br>・早稲田大学入学式<br>・こいのぼり祭り<br>・武者人形<br>・七夕祭り<br>・打ち上げ花火<br>・除夜の鐘つき | 芳賀ライブラリー<br>㈱紀文食品<br>浅草寺<br>和歌山市観光協会<br>㈱吉徳<br>早稲田大学<br>千葉県観光公社<br>㈱吉徳<br>愛知県観光協会<br>広島県観光協会<br>浅草寺 |
| 日 本 の 文 化 | ・歌舞伎（舞台・藤娘・暫）<br>・能・狂言（各1点）<br>・川端康成<br>・「雪国」表紙<br>・大江健三郎<br>・江戸東京博物館外観<br>・江戸日本橋付近（模型）<br>・大倉集古館外観<br>・「夜桜図屏風（部分）」<br>・東京芸術劇場 大ホール<br>・サントリーホール<br>・CDレンタル店 | 松竹株式会社<br>国立能楽堂<br>日本近代文学館<br>日本近代文学館<br>毎日新聞社<br>江戸東京博物館<br>江戸東京博物館<br>大倉集古館（㈶大倉文化財団）<br>大倉集古館（㈶大倉文化財団）<br>東京芸術劇場<br>サントリーホール<br>アコム株式会社 |
| 日本のスポーツ | ・プロ野球「ホームイン」<br>・相撲「土俵上の取組」 | 共同通信フォトサービス<br>共同通信フォトサービス |
| 日 本 の 宗 教 | ・浅草寺本堂と参道 | 浅草寺 |
| 日 本 の 政 治 | ・国会議事堂内部 | 毎日新聞社 |
| 日 本 の 経 済 | ・輸出用自動車積荷風景<br>・自動車生産ライン<br>・証券取引所の取引風景 | トヨタ自動車株式会社<br>トヨタ自動車株式会社<br>東京証券取引所 |
| 日 本 の 産 業 | ・農場風景<br>・ビデオカメラの生産ライン | 東仙北農業共済組合<br>㈱キヤノン |
| 交 通 と 輸 送 | ・新幹線車輌「のぞみ」 | JR東海 |
| 公 害 と 環 境 | ・ゴミの山<br>・立ち枯れた木<br>・放置された古タイヤ | 東京都清掃局<br>共同通信フォトサービス<br>共同通信フォトサービス |
| 日 本 の 歴 史 | ・縄文式土器<br>・弥生式土器<br>・法隆寺西院伽藍<br>・「源氏物語絵巻 柏木三」<br>・文永の役の戦い<br>・徳川家康肖像画<br>・姫路城<br>・参府行列図<br>・東海道五十三次・日本橋<br>・品川海岸を走る蒸気機関車<br>・東京オリンピック<br>・大震災で横倒しになった高速道路 | 東京国立博物館<br>東京国立博物館<br>㈱飛鳥園／法隆寺<br>徳川美術館（㈶徳川黎明会）<br>東京国立博物館<br>徳川美術館（㈶徳川黎明会）<br>姫路市観光協会<br>東京国立博物館<br>東京国立博物館<br>共同通信フォトサービス<br>共同通信フォトサービス<br>毎日新聞社 |

**著　者**

**佐々木瑞枝**（ささき　みずえ）

武蔵野大学文学部・大学院　教授。

著書＝『日本事情』(北星堂書店)、『留学生と見た日本語』(筑摩書房)

『日本語らしい日本語』(研究社出版)、『Dearあなたへ』(リヨン社)、

『日本語教育の教室から―外国人と見た日本事情―』(大修館書店)、

『アカデミック・ジャパニーズ　日本語表現ハンドブックシリーズ』(アルク)、

『日本社会再考』(共著)(北星堂書店)『外国語としての日本語』(講談社現代新書)、

『女と男の日本語辞典 上下巻』(東京堂出版)、『生きた日本語を教える工夫』(小学館)、

『あいまい語辞典』(東京堂出版) 他多数。

英文翻訳：John Millen
　　　　：John Montag
写真撮影：Gillese Espiasse
　　　　：大矢　進
　　　　：富田文雄
デザイン：矢萩典行

# 日本事情入門
View of Today's Japan

1995年8月1日　初版発行　　2006年3月1日　第8刷発行

編　者　アルク日本語書籍編集部
著　者　佐々木瑞枝
発行者　平本照麿
発行所　株式会社アルク
　　　　〒168-8611　東京都杉並区永福2-54-12
　　　　電話　03-3323-5514(日本語書籍編集部)
　　　　　　　03-3327-1101(カスタマーサービス部)
印刷所　図書印刷株式会社

PC:7095491

www.alc.co.jp

# 西暦と日本の年号対照

| 西暦 | 年号 | 西暦 | 年号 | 西暦 | 年号 | 西暦 | 年号 |
|---|---|---|---|---|---|---|---|
| 1900 | 明治 33 | 1932 | 昭和 7 | 1964 | 昭和 39 | 1996 | 平成 8 |
| 1901 | 34 | 1933 | 8 | 1965 | 40 | 1997 | 9 |
| 1902 | 35 | 1934 | 9 | 1966 | 41 | 1998 | 10 |
| 1903 | 36 | 1935 | 10 | 1967 | 42 | 1999 | 11 |
| 1904 | 37 | 1936 | 11 | 1968 | 43 | 2000 | 12 |
| 1905 | 38 | 1937 | 12 | 1969 | 44 | 2001 | 13 |
| 1906 | 39 | 1938 | 13 | 1970 | 45 | | |
| 1907 | 40 | 1939 | 14 | 1971 | 46 | | |
| 1908 | 41 | 1940 | 15 | 1972 | 47 | | |
| 1909 | 42 | 1941 | 16 | 1973 | 48 | | |
| 1910 | 43 | 1942 | 17 | 1974 | 49 | | |
| 1911 | 44 | 1943 | 18 | 1975 | 50 | | |
| 1912 | 大正 1 | 1944 | 19 | 1976 | 51 | | |
| 1913 | 2 | 1945 | 20 | 1977 | 52 | | |
| 1914 | 3 | 1946 | 21 | 1978 | 53 | | |
| 1915 | 4 | 1947 | 22 | 1979 | 54 | | |
| 1916 | 5 | 1948 | 23 | 1980 | 55 | | |
| 1917 | 6 | 1949 | 24 | 1981 | 56 | | |
| 1918 | 7 | 1950 | 25 | 1982 | 57 | | |
| 1919 | 8 | 1951 | 26 | 1983 | 58 | | |
| 1920 | 9 | 1952 | 27 | 1984 | 59 | | |
| 1921 | 10 | 1953 | 28 | 1985 | 60 | | |
| 1922 | 11 | 1954 | 29 | 1986 | 61 | | |
| 1923 | 12 | 1955 | 30 | 1987 | 62 | | |
| 1924 | 13 | 1956 | 31 | 1988 | 63 | | |
| 1925 | 14 | 1957 | 32 | 1989 | 平成 1 | | |
| 1926 | 昭和 1 | 1958 | 33 | 1990 | 2 | | |
| 1927 | 2 | 1959 | 34 | 1991 | 3 | | |
| 1928 | 3 | 1960 | 35 | 1992 | 4 | | |
| 1929 | 4 | 1961 | 36 | 1993 | 5 | | |
| 1930 | 5 | 1962 | 37 | 1994 | 6 | | |
| 1931 | 6 | 1963 | 38 | 1995 | 7 | | |